Daily Warm-Ups

ANALOGIES

Liza Kleinman

Level II

1   2   3   4   5   6   7   8   9   10
ISBN 978-0-8251-6256-5
Copyright © 2007
J. Weston Walch, Publisher
P.O. Box 658 • Portland, Maine 04104-0658
www.walch.com
Printed in the United States of America

The Daily Warm-Ups series is a wonderful way to turn extra classroom minutes into valuable learning time. The 180 quick activities—one for each day of the school year—review, practice, and teach word analogies. These daily activities may be used at the very beginning of class to get students into learning mode, near the end of class to make good educational use of that transitional time, in the middle of class to shift gears between lessons—or whenever else you have minutes that now go unused. In addition to providing students with structure and focus, they are a natural path to other classroom activities involving vocabulary or critical thinking. As students build their vocabularies and become more adept at analogy problem-solving, they will be better prepared for the standardized tests that include analogy problems.

Daily Warm-Ups are easy-to-use reproducibles—simply photocopy the day's activity and distribute it. Or make a transparency of the activity and project it on the board. You may want to use the activities for extra-credit points or as a check on the critical-thinking skills that are built and acquired over time.

However you choose to use them, *Daily Warm-Ups* are a convenient and useful supplement to your regular lesson plans. Make every minute of your class time count!

Daily Warm-Ups: Analogies

What Is an Analogy?

An **analogy** is a statement that shows the logical relationship between two pairs of words.

Example: *Frigid* is to *cold* as *scalding* is to *hot*.

Frigid means extremely *cold*. *Scalding* means extremely *hot*. Each pair of words fits into the same simple sentence that explains the relationship between the words.

Take a look at this analogy:

Cowardly is to *courageous* as _____ is to *arrogant*.

What is the relationship between *cowardly* and *courageous*?

Now choose the correct word to complete the analogy.

(a) angry   (b) humble   (c) passive   (d) insolent

1

What Does an Analogy Look Like?

An analogy generally looks like this:

> digit : finger :: limb : arm

Read the colon (:) as "is to" and the double colon (::) as "as."

In the space below, write the analogy as a sentence.

Now choose the correct word to complete this analogy.

> extortion : crime :: motorcycle : 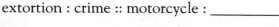 _____

> (a) jailor

> (b) steamboat

> (c) highway

> (d) vehicle

Daily Warm-Ups: Analogies

2

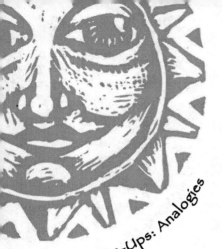

Relationship Sentences

In order to solve an analogy, you need to create a relationship sentence. That's a simple, direct sentence that clearly shows the relationship between the two words.

Write a relationship sentence for the following word pair:

teeth : chew

Now, figure out which of the following word pairs is the correct analogy by plugging each one into the relationship sentence.

(a) hammer : instill

(b) chore : intend

(c) camera : focus

(d) button : fasten

(e) water : invigorate

3

Getting More Specific

Sometimes when you plug in the answer choices, it seems that two or more of the choices work. That means that your relationship sentence wasn't specific enough. When that happens, you need to adjust it.

Suppose your relationship sentence for the word pair *ship : fleet* was this:

> A *ship* is part of a *fleet*.

Now choose the best word pair to complete the analogy.

fleet : ship :: _____ : _____

(a) brim : cap (c) star : constellation
(b) coach : equipment (d) field : grass

Which two choices work with the original relationship sentence?

Write a new, more specific relationship sentence.

Which word pair completes the analogy?

4

Object/Person : Description

One typical analogy relationship is between an object or a person and an adjective that describes that object or person. A word pair in an analogy won't have an adjective that *could* describe the object or person. For example, *cat : striped* is not a good word pair because a cat may or may not be striped. A more typical example is *cat : feline*. A cat is, by definition, feline.

Now choose the best word to complete the analogy.

cat : feline :: dog : _____

(a) furry

(b) obedient

(c) bovine

(d) loyal

(e) canine

5

Agent : Object

This type of analogy pairs up a type of person or thing with an object that is associated with it.

> Example: chef : stove
> A *chef* uses a *stove*.

Of course, a chef might use a lot of things in the course of a day, such as shoes, shampoo, and car keys. The reason why stove pairs with chef in an analogy is that a chef, by definition, uses a stove.

Daily Warm-Ups: Analogies

Choose the correct word from the box to complete the following analogy.

| melody   scale   instrument   podium   performance |

chef : stove :: musician : _____

6

Agent : Action

This type of analogy pairs up a person and the action that the person, by definition, does.

Example: lawyer : litigate

Fill in words to make each of the following an *action : agent* word pair.

judge : _____

teacher : _____

actor : _____

Choose the correct word pair to complete the following analogy.

lawyer : litigate :: _____ : _____

(a) coach : practice

(b) trainer : inspect

(c) detective : mystify

(d) defrauder : cheat

Object : Function

This type of analogy makes a word pair out of a thing and its function—that is, what that thing, by definition, does. For example, a *microscope*, by definition, *magnifies*.

Keep in mind that in a familiar analogy type such as this one, the words might appear in the opposite order, such as *transport : vehicle*.

Write a relationship sentence linking *transport* to *vehicle*. It's okay if the sentence is awkward, as long as it gets the job done.

8

Now complete the following analogy. There is more than one possible correct answer.

transport : vehicle :: _____ : bridge

Object/Description/Action : Greater/ Lesser Degree

This type of analogy pairs something—an object, a description, or an action—with a word that describes something similar, but to a greater or lesser degree.

Write a relationship sentence for each word pair.

ripple : wave   thin : emaciated   race : saunter

Choose the word pair to complete the following analogy.

inconsolable : sad :: _____ : _____

(a) furious : angry

(b) outraged : delighted

(c) overjoyed : overwhelmed

(d) confused : determined

9

Person/Object : Location

This type of analogy compares a person or object to the place where, by definition, that person or object is found.

Example: orator : auditorium

Remember, the relationship can be written in reverse. Write a relationship sentence for this word pair:

theater : performer

Now choose the correct word to complete the following analogy.

climber : mountain :: diver : _____

(a) ocean   (b) dock   (c) oxygen   (d) ship

10

Cause/Effect

In cause/effect analogies, each word pair describes an action and the effect of the action.

Example: impede : obstacle

Write a relationship sentence for this word pair.

Here's a word pair in which the relationship is reversed: *begin : instigated.*

Write a relationship sentence for this word pair.

Now choose the correct word pair to complete the following analogy.

ameliorate : improvement :: _____ : _____

(a) hesitate : decision
(b) agitate : movement
(c) calculate : depletion
(d) infiltrate : destruction
(e) designate : orientation

11

Part : Whole

One typical type of analogy pairs something—such as a person, object, animal, or type of land formation—with the larger group to which it belongs.

> Examples: soldier : battalion
> sheep : herd

Remember, the part and whole can also be in reverse order. The important thing is that both word pairs in the analogy are written in the same order. Here's a word pair written as *whole : part*.

> archipelago : island

Write a relationship sentence for this analogy.

Choose the correct word to complete the following analogy.

stanza : poem :: _____ : essay

(a) topic   (b) persuasion   (c) paragraph   (d) epilogue

12

Object/Person : Category

In this analogy type, something or someone is paired with the category to which it belongs. Remember, the correct answer is not a category to which it may or may not belong. It is the category to which it belongs *by definition*.

Which of the following words would complete this *object: category* word pair?

| turtle | tongue | rodent | serpent |

snake: _____

Choose the correct word pair to complete the following analogy.

juniper : shrub :: _____ : _____

(a) encampment : estrangement

(b) answer : question

(c) mammal : reptile

(d) embellishment : austerity

(e) sister : sibling

Daily Warm-Ups: Analogies

13

Word : Synonym

This type of analogy pairs a word and its synonym (a word meaning the same thing). Try writing some synonyms for these words.

arid : _____

ornate : _____

tumult : _____

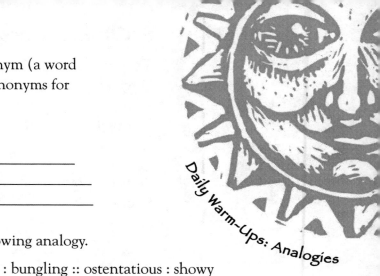

Choose the correct word to complete the following analogy.

_____ : bungling :: ostentatious : showy

(a) cacophonous

(b) entertaining

(c) inept

(d) infallible

(e) replete

14

Word : Antonym

Word : antonym analogies pair a word with another word that means the opposite—its antonym. Try writing some antonyms for these words.

fortitude : _____

dearth : _____

implausible : _____

Complete the following analogy. There may be more than one correct answer.

overpopulated : _____ :: inhibited : unrestrained

15

Parts of Speech

In an analogy, the corresponding words in each pair will be of the same part of speech. In other words, if the first word in one pair is a noun, the first word in the second pair is also a noun. Some words are tricky because they can be more than one part of speech. For example, if you see the word pair *grave : serious*, you might be confused. What does a grave have to do with being serious? Look at the rest of the analogy, though:

> grave : serious :: impulsive : spontaneous

Now you can see that *grave* is an adjective, and this is a basic
> *word : synonym* analogy.

16

Choose the correct word to complete the following analogy.

key : irrelevant :: _____ : clear

(a) lucid

(d) ambiguous

(b) irreverent

(e) undeterred

(c) perennial

Similar, but Different

Sometimes a typical analogy type has a twist that makes it a little bit harder to solve—until you write a relationship sentence. Remember *agent : action* analogies? A typical word pair might be *oracle : foresee*. What would a relationship sentence be for this word pair?

Now look at this one: *oracle : prediction*. *Prediction* isn't an action—it's a noun. Still, even though the part of speech is different from a typical *agent : action* analogy, it's still about what someone, by definition, does. Write a relationship sentence for *oracle: prediction*.

Daily Warm-Ups: Analogies

Choose the correct word pair to complete the following analogy.

translation : interpreter :: _____ : _____

  (a) decision : arbiter   (c) sum : embezzler

  (b) patience : healer   (d) produce : grocer

17

Cheers

Choose the correct word from the box to complete the following analogy.

justification	restoration
adulation	computation
initiation	

laudable : _____ :: odious : condemnation

What relationship sentence did you use to complete this analogy?

18

Choose the correct word to complete the following analogy.

encouragement : deride :: discontent : _____

(a) berate   (b) satisfy   (c) adjourn   (d) verify

What relationship sentence did you use to complete this analogy?

All Talk

Choose the correct word or word pair to complete the following analogies. Then answer the questions.

1. loquacious : speech :: _____ : prose

   (a) abridged   (b) informed   (c) dense   (d) lucid

   What relationship sentence did you use to complete this analogy?

2. monologue : actor :: _____ : _____

   (a) reinforcement : trainer   (d) prank : juvenile

   (b) exhibition : painter   (e) solo : musician

   (c) celebration : successor

What relationship sentence did you use to complete this analogy? Did you have to adjust the sentence?

19

Tough Times

1. Choose the correct word pair to complete the following analogy.

   mourner : lament :: _____ : _____

   (a) hypnotist : deter

   (c) juror : deliberate

   (b) congregant : dispute

   (d) pilgrim : hesitate

What type of analogy is this?

2. Choose the correct word from the box to complete the following analogy.

deteriorate	meditate	infer	contemplate	ingratiate

   value : depreciate :: strength : _____

   What relationship sentence did you use to complete this analogy?

20

Opinions

1. Choose the correct word to complete the following analogy.

   insist : _____ :: abhor : dislike

   (a) refute (b) forget (c) withhold (d) assault (e) suggest

   What relationship sentence did you use to complete this analogy?

   What type of analogy is this?

2. Choose the word from the box to complete the following analogy.

educate eradicate degrade lacerate liberate

   inculpate : blame :: _____ : free

   What relationship sentence did you use to complete this analogy?

   What type of analogy is this?

21

Secrets and Lies

1. Write what each word means in the following analogy. Then write a relationship sentence linking the two words.

   secretive : candor :: _____ : _____

   Now choose the correct word pair to complete the analogy.

   (a) blunt : tact   (c) inimitable : style

   (b) artful : diplomacy   (d) capable : talent

2. Choose the correct word pair to complete the following analogy.

   perjure : prevaricator :: _____ : _____

   (a) illuminate : aide   (c) occupy : tenant

   (b) illustrate : dependent (d) pardon : executioner

   What type of analogy is this?

A Matter of Taste

1. Choose the correct word pair to complete the following analogy.

   sweet : cloying :: _____ : _____

   (a) bitter : acrid   (c) pungent : mild   (e) acidic : basic

   (b) sour : biting   (d) saline : soluble

   What type of analogy is this?

   What relationship sentence did you use to complete this analogy?

2. Choose the correct word from the box to complete the following analogy.

sensation	cognition	color	time

   gustatory : taste :: chronological : _____

   What relationship sentence did you use to complete this analogy?

23

Enough Already

Choose the correct word or word pair to complete the following analogies. Then answer the questions.

1. glutton : gorge :: hedonist : _____

    (a) regret   (c) indulge   (e) endear

    (b) resent   (d) endanger

What type of analogy is this?

What relationship sentence did you use to complete this analogy?

2. limit : infinite :: _____ : amorphous

    (a) validity   (b) meaning   (c) cohesion   (d) shape

What relationship sentence did you use to complete this analogy?

Daily Warm-Ups: Analogies

24

Zzzzzzz

Choose the correct word or word pair to complete the following analogies. Then answer the questions.

1. _____ : hunger :: somnolent : sleep

   (a) fulfilling   (b) disgusting   (c) hesitant   (d) appetizing

At least one choice can be eliminated above because it has nothing to do with hunger. Which choice is that?

What relationship sentence did you use to complete this analogy?

2. monotonous : varied :: _____ : intrepid

   (a) cowardly   (c) unconcerned   (e) bewildered

   (b) internal   (d) impartial

What type of analogy is this?

25

People

Choose the correct word or word pair to complete the following analogies. Then answer the questions.

1. gregarious : extrovert :: jubilant : _____

    (a) protector   (b) celebrant   (c) cleric   (d) juvenile

What type of analogy is this?

2. _____ : _____ :: weaver : tapestry

    (a) balladeer : illusion   (c) raconteur : tale

    (b) composer : conductor   (d) painter : easel

What relationship sentence did you use to complete this analogy?

Daily Warm-Ups: Analogies

26

Stormy Weather

1. Choose the correct word pair to complete the following analogy.

   squall : storm :: _____ : _____

   (a) yelp : vocalization   (c) nod : disagreement

   (b) gesture : hand   (d) shrug : acquiescence

   What relationship sentence did you use to complete this analogy?

   What type of analogy is this?

2. Choose the correct word from the box to complete the following analogy.

sigh	gale	relief	coolant	ocean

   trickle : downpour :: breeze : _____

   What type of analogy is this?

27

Double Your Treasure

Choose the correct word pair to complete the following analogies. Then answer the questions.

1. refuse : treasure :: _____ : _____

   (a) hospitality : organization
   (d) candor : bravado
   (b) shame : pride
   (e) intelligence : confusion
   (c) encouragement : bravery

As it is used in this analogy, what part of speech is *refuse*? What part of speech is *treasure*?

   What type of analogy is this?

2. treasure : memory :: _____ : _____

   (a) insist : truth
   (c) savor : flavor
   (b) register : complaint
   (d) inhale : breath

   What relationship sentence did you use to complete this analogy?

Daily Warm-Ups: Analogies

28

Opposites

1. Choose the correct word from the box to complete the
   following analogy.

exciting	static	lush	incapable	empathetic

   exhilarated : depressed :: _____ : turbulent

   What relationship sentence did you use to complete this analogy?

2. Choose the correct word pair to complete the following analogy.

   wealthy : indigent :: _____ : _____

   (a) hasty : rushed   (d) upset : despondent

   (b) irked : annoyed   (e) competent : blundering

   (c) bewitched : bewildered

Two of the choices have the same relationship sentence. Which ones?

29

War and Peace

Choose the correct word or word pair to complete the following analogies. Then answer the questions.

1. infuriate : anger :: _____ : tranquility

   (a) pacify   (b) perpetuate   (c) capitulate   (d) testify

What type of analogy is this?

2. general : army :: _____ : _____

   (a) weapon : flag (b) captain : team (c) swimmer : pool (d) soldier : troop

What relationship sentence did you use to solve this analogy?

Two of the incorrect answer choices contained words that you might associate with "general" and "army." Which choices were these?

Daily Warm-Ups: Analogies

30

Do It Yourself

What relationship sentence links the two words in the following word pair?

> shelf : storage

What type of analogy is this?

Complete each word pair below to complete the analogy. Remember that the words in both blanks are always nouns.

shelf : storage :: _____ : _____

tent : _____

wall : _____

_____ : cleanliness

31

Synonyms and Antonyms

1. Choose the correct word from the box to complete the following analogy.

| hesitate | exceed | hurry | decrease | ensue |

pursue : follow :: _____ : pause

What type of analogy is this?

2. Choose the correct word to complete the following analogy.

_____ : praise :: mistreatment : kindness

(a) honor

(b) encouragement

(c) invective

(d) commentary

(e) concealment

What type of analogy is this?

32

Power and Money

Choose the correct word or word pair to complete the following analogies. Below each analogy, write the relationship sentence you used.

1. potentate : rule :: _____ : serve

   (a) captain   (b) illusionist   (c) sponsor   (d) lackey

   (If you're not sure of the answer, start by eliminating choices that don't make sense.)

2. beggary : _____ :: seclusion : recluse

   (a) provider   (d) partisan

   (b) mendicant   (e) champion

   (c) enable

33

Odd Relationships

Choose the correct word or word pair to complete the following analogies. Then answer the questions.

1. wan : color :: sluggish : _____

   (a) conviction   (c) confusion   (e) energy

   (b) competition   (d) abrasion

What does *wan* mean?

What relationship sentence did you use to complete this analogy?

34

2. flimsy : fabric :: _____ : meal

   (a) insubstantial   (c) exotic   (e) indescribable

   (b) filling   (d) distasteful

What relationship sentence did you use to complete this analogy?

From Bad to Worse

Choose the correct word pair to complete the following analogies.
Then answer the quetions.

1. _____ : _____ :: selfless : greed

   (a) empathetic : understanding (c) forgetful : illness

   (b) concerned : lewdness (d) mendacious : veracity

What relationship sentence did you use to complete this analogy?

2. _____ : _____ :: jeopardize : endanger

   (a) mitigate : worsen (d) hasten : announce

   (b) impair : judge (e) denounce : revile

   (c) occur : reveal

What type of analogy is this?

If you didn't know the answer, were there any word pairs you could eliminate
right away?

All or Nothing

1. Choose the correct word to complete the following analogy.

   _____ : plenty :: famine : feast

   (a) good (b) repast (c) dearth (d) nuance (e) helping

   What type of analogy is this?

2. Choose the correct word from the box to complete the analogy below.

indigent   celebration   boon   abatement   scarcity

   paucity : _____ :: drought : deluge

36

   What type of analogy is this?

   Were there any words you eliminated right away?

Yea or Nay?

Choose the correct word pair to complete the following analogies. Then answer the questions.

1. zealot : fervent :: _____ : _____

   (a) seer : loquacious

   (d) itinerant : lost

   (b) rebel : obedient

   (e) trickster : duplicitous

   (c) overseer : overwhelmed

What type of analogy is this?

2. _____ : _____ :: speaker : orate

   (a) misanthrope : donate

   (d) facilitator : hasten

   (b) doubter : question

   (e) referee : criticize

   (c) agitator : settle

What type of analogy is this?

What relationship sentence did you use to complete this analogy?

37

© 2007 Walch Publishing

It Could Happen

Choose the correct word to complete the following analogies. Then answer the questions.

1. feasible : _____ :: deliberate : accidental

   (a) fictitious   (d) repetitive

   (b) fantastic   (e) resolved

   (c) knowable

What relationship sentence did you use to complete this analogy?

2. _____ : gravity :: deceptive : trickery

   (a) portentous   (c) contentious   (e) courageous

   (b) pretentious   (d) advantageous

38

Were there any choices that could easily be eliminated right away?

What relationship sentence did you use to complete this analogy?

Feelings

Choose the correct word pair to complete the following analogies. Then answer the questions.

1. wary : terrified :: _____ : _____

   (a) beleaguered : confident   (c) interested : obsessed

   (b) overloaded : lacking   (d) endearing : lovely

What type of analogy is this?

2. repent : remorseful :: _____ : _____

   (a) partake : encumbered   (d) reveal : relevant

   (b) infer : confused   (e) describe : written

   (c) refuse : abstinent

What relationship sentence did you use to complete this analogy?

39

Better and Worse

Choose the correct word to complete the following analogies.
Then answer the questions.

1. improve : flag :: _____ : diminish

   (a) increase   (b) lessen   (c) demolish   (d) unravel

What part of speech is *flag* in this question? How do you know?

What type of analogy is this?

2. erode : land :: discourage : _____

   (a) commitment   (b) influence   (c) aid   (d) resolve

This analogy is not one of the common types. What relationship sentence
did you use to complete this analogy?

Eat and Run

1. Choose the correct word pair to complete the following analogy.

   grazing : pasture :: _____ : _____

   (a) eating : plate   (c) reading : library

   (b) strolling : lawn   (d) enumerating : calculator

What relationship sentence did you use to complete this analogy?

2. Choose the correct word from the box to complete the following analogy.

stage	curtain	soliloquy	monologue	cast

   musicians : ensemble :: actors : _____

What relationship sentence did you use to complete this analogy?

Which two answer choices have similar enough meanings that you could eliminate both?

41

Top and Bottom

Choose the correct word or word pair to complete the following analogies. Then answer the questions.

1. _____ : pinnacle :: penetrate : core

   (a) review   (c) cede   (e) attempt

   (b) scale   (d) comprehend

What relationship sentence did you use to complete this analogy?

2. footnote : chapter :: _____ : _____

   (a) imprint : volume   (d) author : revision

   (b) margin : page   (e) postscript : letter

   (c) message : bottle

What relationship sentence did you use to complete it? Did you need to revise your relationship sentence after you looked at the choices?

42

Daily Warm-Ups: Analogies

Matching

Match each word pair to the one that completes the analogy, and write the correct letter on the line.

___ 1. spurious : false ::

___ 2. puerile : mature ::

___ 3. ignite : conflagration ::

___ 4. worker : staff ::

(a) demolish : destruction

(b) player : team

(c) opulent : wealthy

(d) naïve : worldly

What type was each analogy?

1. _____

2. _____

3. _____

4. _____

43

Looking Sharp

Choose the correct word to complete the following analogies. Then answer the questions.

1. obtuse : sharp :: _____ : opaque

   (a) convoluted   (c) transparent   (e) ebullient

   (b) paradoxical   (d) immoveable

What relationship sentence did you use to complete this analogy?

2. acute : vision :: honed : _____

   (a) skill   (b) impression   (c) personality   (d) knowledge

Is this one of the common analogy types? If so, which one?

What relationship sentence did you use to complete this analogy?

Daily Warm-Ups: Analogies

44

Don't Stare!

Choose the correct word or word pair to complete the following analogies. Then answer the questions.

1. peek : ogle :: _____ : _____

   (a) stagger : waddle   (c) insinuate : imply

   (b) murmur : shout   (d) renege : offer

What relationship sentence did you use to complete this analogy?

2. visualize : see :: iterate : _____

   (a) believe   (c) confiscate   (e) say

   (b) deliver   (d) think

What type of analogy is this?

45

Busybody

1. Choose the correct word to complete the following analogy.

   _____ : interfere :: assailant : attack

   (a) applicant   (c) jingoist   (e) ingrate

   (b) meddler   (d) infidel

Is this one of the common analogy types? If so, which one?

What relationship sentence did you use to complete this analogy?

Daily Warm-Ups: Analogies

2. Choose the correct word from the box to complete the following analogy.

profane	engorged	hobbled	ambient	detailed

   corpulent : lithe :: _____ : cursory

   What relationship sentence did you use to complete this analogy?

46

Give It a Chance

Choose the correct word or word pair to complete the following analogies. Then answer the questions.

1. pacifist : fighting :: purist : _____

    (a) hydration   (c) filtration   (e) expectation

    (b) incarceration   (d) adulteration

What is a pacifist?

What relationship sentence did you use to complete this analogy?

2. pie : wedge :: _____ : _____

    (a) cake : confection   (c) décor : interior

    (b) beverage : carbonation   (d) pizza : slice

What type of analogy is this?

What relationship sentence did you use to complete this analogy?

47

Hungry

Choose the correct word or word pair to complete the following analogies. Then answer the questions.

1. slake : thirst :: _____ : hunger

   (a) satiate   (c) besiege   (e) acquiesce

   (b) determine   (d) devour

Are there any choices you can eliminate right away because they have no relationship to *hunger*?

What relationship sentence did you use to complete this analogy?

48

2. rapacious : ravenous :: _____ : _____

   (a) incessant : frequent   (c) indifferent : impartial

   (b) endearing : irritating   (d) negligible : consequential

If you aren't sure what the words in the question pair mean, are there any answer choices you can eliminate right away?

© 2007 Walch Publishing

Clouds

Choose the correct word or word pair to complete the following analogies. Below each analogy, write the relationship sentence you used.

1. obfuscate : confusion :: demarcate : _____

   (a) sundries   (c) capers   (e) boundaries

   (b) canopies   (d) raptures

2. foreboding : misfortune :: _____ : _____

   (a) optimism : luck   (d) cynicism : wit

   (b) wariness : stealth   (e) skepticism : knowledge

   (c) commencement : end

49

More Matching

Match each word pair to the pair that has the same relationship, and write the correct letter on the line.

___ 1. caper : adventure

___ 2. cattle : herd

___ 3. dabble : delve

___ 4. orator : podium

(a) blade : tuft

(b) skim : study

(c) captain : helm

(d) mixture : mélange

50

What relationship sentence did you use to complete each analogy?

1. _____

2. _____

3. _____

4. _____

Notions

1. Choose the correct word pair to complete the following analogy.

   paragon : ideal :: _____ : _____

   (a) pariah : amity

   (b) palliative : irritant

   (c) paradox : contradiction

   (d) panorama : installation

   (e) panacea : health

   What type of analogy is this?

   Were there any answer choices that you could eliminate right away?

2. Write a word on the line to complete the following analogy. There is more than one possible correct answer.

   ruminate : ponder :: _____ : revere

   What part of speech is the word that completes the analogy?

   What relationship sentence did you use to complete this analogy?

51

Touching

Choose the correct word or word pair to complete the following analogies. Then answer the questions.

1. _____ : _____ :: tactile : touch

    (a) sensory : enjoyment   (c) sweet : taste

    (b) obstructed : vision   (d) olfactory : smell

What relationship sentence did you use to complete this analogy?

Were there any answer choices you could eliminate right away?

2. tenuous : grasp :: _____ : understanding

    (a) informed   (b) shaky   (c) imaginative   (d) nuanced

What relationship sentence did you use to link the first word pair?

52

Get to the Point

Choose the correct word or word pair to complete the following analogies. Then answer the questions.

1. succinct : verbose :: _____ : _____

   (a) unruly : chaotic   (c) impervious : vulnerable

   (b) bereaved : alive   (d) credible : gullible

What relationship sentence did you use to complete this analogy?

Were there any answer choices you could eliminate right away because the words in the pair have no clear relationship?

2. direction : compass :: _____ : _____

   (a) darkness : curtain   (c) depth : water

   (b) pressure : barometer   (d) weight : barbell

What relationship sentence did you use to complete this analogy?

A Riot

Choose the correct word pair to complete the following analogies.
Then answer the questions.

1. _____ : _____ :: incite : riot

   (a) ignite : fire   (d) enchant : evening

   (b) inflame : wound   (e) arrange : event

   (c) embrace : idea

What type of analogy is this?

What relationship sentence did you use to complete this analogy?

2. chuckle : guffaw :: _____ : _____

   (a) sigh : remember   (c) grin : giggle   (e) frown : grimace

   (b) simper : sulk   (d) weep : mourn

What type of analogy is this?

54

Crime Doesn't Pay

Choose the correct word to complete the following analogies.
Then answer the questions.

1. shoplifting : theft :: _____ : deception

    (a) improving   (c) belief   (e) agreement

    (b) insolence   (d) lying

What relationship sentence did you use to complete this analogy?

2. _____ : searchers :: band : pirates

    (a) objective   (b) treasure   (c) portion   (d) flashlight   (e) posse

What type of analogy is this?

What relationship sentence did you use to complete this analogy?

55

Perfect Harmony

1. Choose two words from the box to complete the following analogy.

inform	implore	undo	instruct
believe	praise	belittle	plead

include : ostracize :: _____ : _____

What type of analogy is this?

2. Choose the correct word pair to complete the following analogy.

_____ : _____ :: note : tune

(a) music : art   (c) painter : artist   (e) word : sentence

(b) clay : sculpture   (d) entrepreneur : business

What relationship sentence did you use to complete this analogy? Did you have to revise your relationship sentence? If so, how?

56

Blame Game

Choose the correct word or word pair to complete the following analogies. Then answer the questions.

1. scapegoat : blame :: hero : _____

    (a) perform

    (b) admire

    (c) condemn

    (d) belie

    (e) resuscitate

    What relationship sentence did you use to complete this analogy?

2. prosecutor : accuse :: _____ : _____

    (a) jury : select

    (b) defendant : deny

    (c) judge : opine

    (d) witness : infer

What type of analogy type is this?

57

Sweet Nothings

Choose the correct word pair to complete the following analogies.
Then answer the questions.

1. saccharine : sweet :: _____ : _____

   (a) livid : annoyed (c) acrimonious : blunt

   (b) sour : bitter   (d) lofty : ideal

What relationship sentence did you use to complete this analogy?

2. _____ : _____ :: censor : delete

   (a) artist : indulge   (d) satirist : lampoon

   (b) procrastinator : hasten (e) interpreter : exaggerate

   (c) prevaricator : learn

What type of analogy is this?

What relationship sentence did you use to complete this analogy?

58

Take Off

1. Choose the correct word pair to complete the following analogy.

   launch : investigation :: _____ : _____

   (a) initiate : proceedings   (c) insinuate : statement

   (b) imperil : data   (d) illustrate : point

   What relationship sentence did you use to complete this analogy?

2. Complete the following analogy with a word pair from the box.

envision : realize	obscure : clarify	pontificate : reiterate
torment : tease	escalate : decelerate	

   _____ : _____ :: lop : trim

What type of analogy is this?

59

Being Green

Choose the correct word or word pair to complete the following analogies. Below each analogy, write the relationship sentence you used.

1. neophyte : seasoned :: _____ : _____

   (a) cynic : hardened   (c) sovereign : overreaching

   (b) proprietor : indebted   (d) pragmatist : unrealistic

2. verdant : lush :: precarious : _____

   (a) stealthy   (b) risky   (c) precocious   (d) languid

What Type?

Match each word pair to the analogy type that describes it. Write the correct letter on the line.

Word Pairs

___ 1. dancers : troupe

___ 2. sad : devastated

___ 3. acerbic : caustic

___ 4. professor : classroom

___ 5. painter : canvas

___ 6. muse : inspire

___ 7. effusive : terse

___ 8. oboist : musician

Types of Analogy

(a) agent : object

(b) description : greater degree

(c) part : whole

(d) person : location

(e) word : synonym

(f) agent : action

(g) person : category

(h) word : antonym

61

Contradictions

Choose the correct word or word pair to complete the following analogies. Then answer the questions.

1. paradox : contradictory :: _____ : soothing

   (a) placebo   (c) balm   (e) totem

   (b) irritant   (d) talisman

What relationship sentence did you use to complete this analogy?

What type of analogy is this?

62

2. histrionic : unemotional :: _____ : _____

   (a) proficient : unskilled   (c) rapid : diminishing

   (b) ambient : musical   (d) ungracious : demeaning

   What type of analogy is this?

Cold and Gray

1. Choose the correct word pair to complete the following analogy.

   sleet : precipitation :: _____ : _____

   (a) tedium : transformation   (d) surfeit : famine

   (b) perambulation : movement   (e) eloquence : speech

   (c) knowledge : reiteration

2. Choose the correct word from the box to complete the following analogy.

clashing	vibrant	pigmented	contrasting	mellowing

   discordant : tones :: _____ : colors

Is this analogy one of the common types?

What relationship sentence did you use to complete this analogy?

63

Be Afraid

Choose the correct word or word pair to complete the following analogies. Below each analogy, write the relationship sentence you used.

Daily Warm-Ups: Analogies

1. _____ : _____ :: temerity : coward

   (a) indolence : offender

   (b) candor : thief

   (c) conviviality : misanthrope

   (d) respectability : congregant

   (e) encouragement : supporter

64

2. threat : _____ :: statement : baseless

   (a) idle   (b) perceived   (c) implied   (d) egregious   (e) insidious

Sticking Point

Choose the correct word or word pair to complete the following analogies. Below each analogy, write what type of analogy it is and the relationship sentence you used.

1. adhere : glue :: _____ : _____

   (a) interpret : speech   (c) arrange : encampment

   (b) rectify : hammer   (d) divide : barrier

2. sycophant : toady :: adversary : _____

   (a) embezzler   (c) ingrate   (e) helpmate

   (b) foe   (d) consumer

65

Peace

Choose the correct word pair to complete the following analogies. Then answer the questions.

1. antebellum : war :: _____ : _____

   (a) antisocial : education

   (b) prenatal : birth

   (c) preventative : accident

   (d) bellicose : peace

What relationship sentence did you use to complete this analogy?

2. _____ : _____ :: pester : plague

   (a) frighten : terrify

   (b) congregate : segregate

   (c) exhort : deny

   (d) exhume : bury

   (e) regress : proceed

66

What type of relationship does this analogy use?

Water, Water Everywhere

Choose the correct word or word pair to complete the following analogies. Then answer the questions.

1. hydrate : water :: _____ : _____

   (a) syndicate : symphony

   (d) ennoble : anecdote

   (b) educate : masses

   (e) deride : supporter

   (c) bolster : column

   What relationship sentence did you use to complete this analogy?

   What type of analogy is this?

2. titanic : immense :: innocuous : _____

   (a) unoriginal (b) palatable (c) rotund (d) nihilistic (e) harmless

What type of analogy is this?

Were there any answer choices you were able to eliminate immediately?

67

Which One?

Choose the word or word pair that does NOT correctly complete the following analogies. Then answer the questions.

1. candid : reveal :: _____ : _____

   (a) patient : endure   (d) anxious : implore

   (b) inquisitive : wonder   (e) accusatory : impugn

   (c) reminiscent : remind

What relationship sentence did you use to complete this analogy?

Daily Warm-Ups: Analogies

2. refined : boorish :: prejudiced : _____

   (a) impartial   (b) unbiased   (c) preconceived   (d) disinterested

   What relationship sentence did you use to link the word pair in the question?

   What type of analogy is this?

68

Secret Club

1. Choose the correct word to complete the following analogy.

    miserly : benefactor :: _____ : realist

    (a) quintessential   (c) questionable

    (b) quixotic   (d) querulous

    What relationship sentence did you use to complete this analogy?

2. Choose the correct word from the box to complete the following analogy.

leaders	clergy	adherents	doctrines	dogmas

    sect : _____ :: clan : members

What relationship sentence did you use to complete this analogy? Did you need to revise your relationship sentence?

69

Innocent Until Proven Guilty

Choose the correct word or word pair to complete the following analogies. Below each analogy, write the relationship sentence you used.

1. inculpate : exoneration :: _____ : _____

   (a) replicate : defamation

   (b) incarcerate : liberation

   (c) indicate : manifestation

   (d) speculate : infestation

   (e) meditate : restoration

70

2. Choose the word that completes this analogy.

   naïf : jaded :: connoisseur : _____

   (a) ignorant (b) impressed (c) unruly (d) trusting (e) discerning

Flying Objects

Choose the correct word or word pair to complete the following analogies. Below each analogy, write what type of analogy it is and the relationship sentence you used.

1. birds : aviary :: _____ : _____

   (a) applicants : pool   (c) conservationists : zoo

   (b) dissenters : belief   (d) flora : greenhouse

2. aviator : flight :: _____ : investigation

   (a) suspect   (c) sleuth   (e) instigator

   (b) private   (d) entrepreneur

71

Your Roots Are Showing

Complete the following two analogies. Use your knowledge of word roots to help you decode words that are unfamiliar to you. Then answer the questions.

1. agoraphobia : fear :: _____ : _____

    (a) oligarchy : government

    (c) justice : trial

    (b) penalty : competition

    (d) cognition : behavior

What relationship sentence did you use to complete this analogy?

What type of analogy is this?

2. juvenescence : age :: _____ : _____

    (a) imagination : folly

    (c) perpetuation : limit

    (b) indulgence : repast

    (d) infiltration: investigation

What relationship sentence did you use to complete this analogy?

Stop, Thief!

Choose the correct word or word pair to complete the following analogies. Then answer the questions.

pilfer : goods :: _____ : _____

(a) embrace : identity   (d) deduct : deposit

(b) embezzle : funds   (e) encounter : security

(c) usurp : accounts

This analogy is not one of the common types. What relationship sentence did you use to link the word pair in the question?

2. thwart : frustrate :: endorse : _____

(a) reveal   (b) instill   (c) recall   (d) impair   (e) support

What type of analogy is this?

73

Hotheaded

1. Choose the correct word from the box to complete the following analogy.

| enraged defaming flammable controversial embellished |

irascible : temper :: _____ : material

What relationship sentence did you use to complete this analogy?

2. Select the word pair that completes the analogy.

_____ : _____ :: incendiary : inflammatory

(a) indelible : fleeting

(d) engulfing : endangering

(b) credible : argumentative

(e) unique : unusual

(c) puerile : childish

What relationship sentence did you use to complete this analogy?

What type of analogy is this?

74

Stories

Choose the correct word or word pair to complete the following analogies. Then answer the questions.

1. fable : tale :: _____ : _____

   (a) endeavor : art   (d) insinuation : logic

   (b) chantey : song   (e) syntax : punctuation

   (c) education : university

   What relationship sentence did you use to complete this analogy?

   What type of analogy is this?

2. credulous : _____ :: lithe : flexibility

   (a) capability   (b) gullibility   (c) agility   (d) utility

   What relationship sentence did you use to complete this analogy?

75

© 2007 Walch Publishing

Pure and Simple

Choose the correct word or word pair to complete the following analogies. Then answer the questions.

1. cleanse : _____ :: clarify : confusion

    (a) impurity

    (d) incongruity

    (b) derision

    (e) penance

    (c) detergent

What relationship sentence did you use to complete this analogy?

2. ascetic : austerity :: _____ : _____

    (a) pedagogue : ignorance

    (d) spectator : individuality

    (b) transient : permanence

    (e) pauper : indigence

    (c) agitator : peculiarity

What relationship sentence did you use to complete this analogy?

Which type of analogy is this?

76

Can't Touch This

Choose the correct word or word pair to complete the following analogies. Then answer the questions.

1. intangible : touch :: implacable : _____

   (a) anticipate   (d) soothe

   (b) deprecate   (e) meld

   (c) impugn

   What relationship sentence did you use to complete this analogy?

2. affecting : response :: _____ : _____

   (a) mesmerizing : trickery   (c) insidious : understanding

   (b) unsettling : agitation   (d) cavernous : exploration

   What relationship sentence did you use to complete this analogy?

   What type of analogy is this?

77

Fighting

1. Choose the correct word from the box to complete the following analogy.

| facilitate | congeal | embark | satiate | display | preserve |

pugilist : fight :: conservationist : _____

What relationship sentence did you use to complete this analogy?

What type of analogy is this?

2. Choose the correct word pair to complete the following analogy.

_____ : _____ :: disputant : accord

(a) student : tutelage   (d) malcontent : complaint

(b) deviant : behavior   (e) adversary : conflict

(c) sage : ignorance

What relationship sentence did you use to complete this analogy?

Which two incorrect answer choices have the same relationship sentence?

78

Parts

Choose the correct word or word pair to complete the following analogies. Then answer the questions.

1. serial : installment :: _____ : _____

   (a) process : step   (c) condition : diagnosis

   (b) value : virtue   (d) solution : problem

What relationship sentence did you use to complete this analogy?

What type of analogy is this?

2. intricate : pattern :: _____ : description

   (a) misleading (b) deliberate (c) fanciful (d) detailed (e) terse

What relationship sentence did you use to complete this analogy?

79

Fear and Loathing

Choose the correct word pair to complete the following analogies.
Then answer the questions.

1. coward : intrepid :: _____ : _____

   (a) donor : benevolent

   (d) plagiarist : infamous

   (b) expatriate : adventurous

   (e) novice : weathered

   (c) interloper : welcome

What relationship sentence did you use to complete this analogy?

2. dislike : revile :: _____ : _____

   (a) understand : disbelieve

   (c) misapprehend : approximate

   (b) request : insist

   (d) belie : support

What relationship type is this analogy?

80

Still Hungry

Choose the correct word pair to complete the following analogies.
Then answer the questions.

1. _____ : _____ :: gourmand : excess

   (a) interpreter : fastidiousness   (c) narrator : verbosity

   (b) indigent : poverty   (d) merchant : success

What relationship sentence did you use to complete this analogy?

What type of analogy is this?

2. knife : incise :: _____ : _____

   (a) clamp : secure   (c) wrench : instill   (e) bludgeon : sharpen

   (b) awl : bind   (d) cable : install

What type of analogy is this?

81

Lively

Choose the correct word or word pair to complete the following analogies. Then answer the questions.

1. animated : lethargy :: peaceable : _____

   (a) reluctance　　　(d) truculence

   (b) diligence　　　(e) decadence

   (c) impudence

What relationship sentence did you use to complete this analogy?

2. vim : energy :: _____ : _____

   (a) sagaciousness : wisdom　　　(d) insistence : inquisitiveness

   (b) embarrassment : dignity　　　(e) conviction : misdemeanor

   (c) impairment : enhancement

What relationship sentence did you use to complete this analogy?

What type of analogy is this?

82

Boring

1. Choose the correct word pair to complete the following analogy.

   somnolent : invigorating :: _____ : _____

   (a) endearing : preferred   (d) intrusive : disturbing

   (b) sinister : malevolent   (e) contagious : transmittable

   (c) toxic : wholesome

   What relationship sentence did you use to complete this analogy?

2. Choose the word pair that does NOT correctly complete the following analogy.

   awl : bore :: _____ : _____

   (a) vehicle : transport   (c) cable : connect   (e) fence : enclose

   (b) value : instill   (d) yardstick : measure

   What relationship sentence did you use to complete this analogy?

   What type of analogy is this?

83

Misunderstandings

Choose the correct word pair to complete the following analogies.
Then answer the questions.

1. imbroglio : tiff :: _____ : _____

   (a) annex : building

   (c) conflagration : flame

   (b) compassion : disregard

   (d) provocation : resolution

What relationship sentence did you use to complete this analogy?

What type of analogy is this?

84

2. _____ : _____ :: incognito : identity

   (a) encoded : information

   (d) monochromatic : color

   (b) predictable : future

   (e) symbolic : allegory

   (c) convoluted : road

What relationship sentence did you use to complete this analogy?

Land and Sea

1. Choose the correct word from the box to complete the following analogy.

accrue	defame	corrode	abdicate	oxidize	decant

erode : land :: _____ : metal

What relationship sentence did you use to complete this analogy?

2. Choose the correct word pair to complete the following analogy.

saline : brine :: _____ : _____

(a) illusory : story

(b) irreplaceable : comrade

(c) inflammatory : remark

(d) deprecating : humor

(e) urban : metropolis

What relationship sentence did you use to complete this analogy?

What type of analogy is this?

85

Large Appetite

Choose the correct word or word pair to complete the following analogies. Below each analogy, write the relationship sentence you used.

1. satiate : appetite :: _____ : _____

    (a) sublimate : desire

    (b) quench : thirst

    (c) endure : hardship

    (d) designate : falsehood

    (e) deign : exhaustion

86

2. edible : fare :: _____ : water

    (a) prodigious   (b) refreshing   (c) odious   (d) potable   (e) translucent

Order!

Choose the correct word or word pair to complete the following analogies. Below each analogy, write the relationship sentence you used.

1. chaos : pandemonium :: _____ : _____

   (a) invective : vituperation

   (d) negligence : attention

   (b) malfeasance : plot

   (e) charisma : management

   (c) disdain : obsequiousness

2. chronology : event :: bibliography : _____

   (a) composition (b) library (c) index (d) dissertation (e) source

87

Giving

Choose the correct word or word pair to complete the following analogies. Below each analogy, write the relationship sentence you used.

1. miser : munificent :: potentate : _____

   (a) benevolent   (c) powerless   (e) prolific

   (b) instrumental   (d) imperial

2. philanthropist : benefactor :: _____ : _____

   (a) misogynist : recluse   (c) despot : prisoner

   (b) misanthrope : catalyst   (d) infidel : heretic

88

Beliefs

1. Choose the correct word pair to complete the following analogy.

_____ : _____ :: inchoate : opinion

(a) ingrained : tenet   (c) changeable : weather

(b) vague : idea   (d) malleable : mind

What relationship sentence did you use to complete this analogy?

2. Choose the correct word from the box to complete the following analogy.

| conviction | restitution | inundation | ordinance | intelligence |

blasphemy : gospel :: _____ : doubt

What type of analogy is this?

89

Handy Exercise

Match each of the following word pairs to the one that is analogous.
Write the correct letter on the line.

____ 1. dexterous : hands

____ 2. surprised : stunned

____ 3. spark : ignite

____ 4. impede : facilitate

____ 5. paucity : dearth

(a) rile : appease

(b) confused : bewildered

(c) adroit : mind

(d) plethora : array

(e) brake : stop

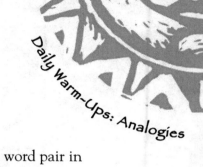

Write the relationship sentence you formed to link each word pair in
the left column above.

1. _____

2. _____

3. _____

4. _____

5. _____

90

Fill in the Blank

Complete each of the following analogies by writing a word on the line. There may be more than one correct answer for each analogy.

1. timid : bold :: _____ : generous

2. bureaucrat : government :: _____ : team

3. spacious : cavernous :: energetic : _____

4. poignant : touching :: grueling : _____

5. fractious : docile :: fragrant : _____

91

Good Behavior

Choose the correct word or word pair to complete the following analogies. Then answer the questions.

1. expunge : memory :: eradicate : _____

   (a) existence

   (d) resistance

   (b) agreement

   (e) impairment

   (c) importance

What relationship sentence did you use to complete this analogy?

2. discriminating : epicure :: _____ : _____

   (a) esoteric : omnivore

   (c) boorish : esthete

   (b) decrepit : athlete

   (d) erudite : scholar

   What relationship sentence did you use to complete this analogy?

   What type of analogy is this?

Daily Warm-Ups: Analogies

92

Land and Sea

Choose the correct word or word pair to complete the following analogies. Then answer the questions.

1. buoy : float :: _____ : _____

    (a) terminal : depart

    (b) beacon : mislead

    (c) journey : undertake

    (d) bolster : resonate

    (e) trestle : support

    What relationship sentence did you use to complete this analogy?

    What type of analogy is this?

2. familiar : exotic :: succinct : _____

    (a) emboldened   (c) tawdry   (e) pithy

    (b) indistinct   (d) wordy

    What relationship sentence did you use to complete this analogy?

    What type of analogy is this?

93

Pretty Please

Choose the correct word pair to complete the following analogies.
Then answer the questions.

1. cajole : wheedle :: _____ : _____

    (a) exonerate : absolve   (c) vindicate : exculpate

    (b) indicate : coordinate   (d) harass : hamper

What relationship sentence did you use to complete this analogy?

2. fop : vanity :: _____ : _____

    (a) antagonist : sympathy   (d) ambassador : dignity

    (b) captive : liberty   (e) transient : efficiency

    (c) virtuoso : talent

What relationship sentence did you use to complete this analogy?

What type of analogy is this?

94

Climb Every Mountain

Choose the correct word or word pair to complete the following analogies. Then answer the questions.

1. apex : nadir :: _____ : confidence

   (a) contempt   (c) veracity   (e) recalcitrance

   (b) trepidation   (d) indulgence

   What relationship sentence did you use to complete this analogy?

2. mesa : formation :: _____ : _____

   (a) accusation : respite   (c) anecdote : story

   (b) tower : view   (d) embankment : river

What relationship sentence did you use to complete this analogy?

What type of analogy is this?

95

Labor

Choose the correct word or word pair to complete the following analogies. Then answer the questions.

Daily Warm-Ups: Analogies

1. _____ : _____ :: prolific : writer

   (a) descriptive : passage   (d) cumulative : effect

   (b) fertile : land   (e) estranged : relative

   (c) invasive : plant

What relationship sentence did you use to complete this analogy?

2. procrastination : shirker :: _____ : dictator

   (a) infatuation   (b) adulation   (c) iteration   (d) domination

What relationship sentence did you use to complete this analogy?

What type of analogy is this?

96

Home Improvements

Choose the correct word or word pair to complete the following analogies. Then answer the questions.

1. decorate : adornment :: _____ : _____

   (a) enhance : reflection

   (d) expunge : eraser

   (b) disregard : announcement

   (e) prohibit : edict

   (c) tend : propensity

   What relationship sentence did you use to complete this analogy?

   What type of analogy is this?

2. raze : building :: _____ : population

   (a) multiply

   (c) survey

   (e) decimate

   (b) inhibit

   (d) remonstrate

   What relationship sentence did you use to complete this analogy?

97

Opinionated

1. Choose the correct word from the box to complete the analogy.

| reserve | relegate | reprise | remonstrate | recall |

recant : opinion :: _____ : product

What relationship sentence did you use to complete this analogy?

2. Choose the correct word pair to complete the following analogy.

_____ : _____ :: opine : belief

(a) falsify : query   (d) enunciate : slur

(b) repeat : statement   (e) delineate : argument

(c) inform : fact

What relationship sentence did you use to complete this analogy?

98

Get It?

Choose the correct word or word pair to complete the following analogies. Below each analogy, write the relationship sentence you used.

1. tenuous : hold :: _____ : _____

   (a) uncompromised : health   (c) sullied : morals

   (b) weak : understanding   (d) unflagging : strength

2. _____ : escapade :: jester : prankster

   (a) caper   (b) cavalcade   (c) calibration   (d) cameo   (e) cacophony

Daily Warm-Ups: Analogies

99

© 2007 Walch Publishing

Moody

Choose the correct word or word pair to complete the following analogies. Then answer the questions.

1. _____ : _____ :: curmudgeon : disgruntled

   (a) nonagenarian : youthful   (c) candidate : officious

   (b) ambassador : brusque   (d) bigot : biased

What relationship sentence did you use to complete this analogy?

Is this one of the common analogy types? If so, which one?

2. glum : despondent :: interested : _____

   (a) impartial   (c) maniacal   (d) unambiguous

   (b) lackadaisical   (e) obsessed

What relationship sentence did you use to complete this analogy?

What type of analogy is this?

100

Endeavors

Choose the correct word pair to complete the following analogies. Then answer the questions.

1. theologian : religion :: _____ : _____

   (a) geologist : adventure

   (c) oracle : prediction

   (b) anthropologist : culture

   (d) villain : malfeasance

What relationship sentence did you use to complete this analogy?

Were there any wrong answer choices that you were able to eliminate immediately?

2. _____ : _____ : embezzlement : fund

   (a) plagiarism : idea

   (d) fraud : compensation

   (b) libel : slander

   (e) misrepresentation : deliberation

   (c) blackmail : victim

What relationship sentence did you use to complete this analogy?

101

Deadly

Choose the correct word or word pair to complete the following analogies. Then answer the questions.

1. sloth : torpidity :: _____ : _____

    (a) gluttony : satisfaction   (c) greed : avarice

    (b) pride: shame   (d) wrath : benevolence

What relationship sentence did you use to complete this analogy?

What type of analogy is this?

2. mortal : wound :: _____ : disease

    (a) congenital (b) recurring (c) rare (d) fatal (e) benign

    What relationship sentence did you use to complete this analogy?

102

Bookish

Choose the correct word or word pair to complete the following analogies. Below each analogy, write what type of analogy it is and the relationship sentence you used.

1. pamphlet : tome :: _____ : _____

   (a) rainbow : spectrum   (d) sketch : painting

   (b) prism : light   (e) ditty : symphony

   (c) endorsement : recommendation

2. bibliophile : books :: _____ : food

   (a) consumer (b) gourmand (c) omnivore (d) sophisticate (e) chef

© 2007 Walch Publishing

You Complete Me

Complete the following analogies. There may be more than one correct answer for each.

1. sporadic : predictable :: _____ : serious

2. vehement : fervent :: indifferent : _____

3. vagrant : wander :: monarch : _____

4. confident : brazen :: frugal : _____

5. inter : unearth :: hoard : _____

What relationship sentence did you use to complete each analogy?

1. _____

2. _____

3. _____

4. _____

5. _____

104

Back Talk

Choose the correct word or word pair to complete the following analogies. Then answer the questions.

1. repeal : law :: _____ : license

   (a) restrain   (d) revoke

   (b) reconstitute   (e) relish

   (c) reconnoiter

What relationship sentence did you use to complete this analogy?

2. _____ : _____ :: saucy : impudent

   (a) lively : vivacious   (d) encumbered : bereft

   (b) deleterious : helpful   (e) rosy : pallid

   (c) indeterminate : focused

What relationship sentence did you use to complete this analogy?

What type of analogy is this?

105

Party People

Choose the correct word pair to complete the following analogy.
Then answer the questions.

delegate : representation :: _____ : _____

(a) surrogate : implication   (c) commentator : explanation

(b) combatant : pacification   (d) captor : liberation

What relationship sentence did you use to complete this analogy?

What type of analogy is this?

What part of speech is *delegate* in this analogy?

Serpents

Choose the correct word pair to complete the following analogies.
Then answer the questions.

1. serpentine : river :: _____ : _____

   (a) ponderous : volume   (d) ill-conceived : notion

   (b) rambling : speech   (e) sea-worthy : vessel

   (c) foolish : investment

   What relationship sentence did you use to complete this analogy?

2. _____ : _____ :: asp : snake

   (a) diamond : gem   (c) penitence : reward

   (b) grammar : punctuation   (d) bed : chrysanthemum

What relationship sentence did you use to complete this analogy?

What type of analogy is this?

107

Pedigree

Choose the correct word or word pair to complete the following analogies. Below each analogy, write the relationship sentence you used.

1. _____ : ape :: bovine : cow

    (a) porcine
    (b) mammalian
    (c) simian
    (d) intelligent
    (e) endangered

108

2. pedigree : lineage :: _____ : _____

    (a) descendant : inheritance
    (b) matriarch : patriarch
    (c) hierarchy : anarchy
    (d) ancestor : forebear
    (e) root : branch

Concentrate

Choose the correct word or word pair to complete the following analogies. Then answer the questions.

1. concentrated : dilute :: _____ : defiant

   (a) detrimental   (d) punctual

   (b) impudent   (e) deferential

   (c) courageous

What relationship sentence did you use to complete this analogy?

What part of speech is *concentrated* in this analogy?

2. glance : pore :: _____ : _____

   (a) induce : trigger   (c) praise : inveigh

   (b) nibble : devour   (d) endure : slog

What relationship sentence did you use to complete this analogy?

109

Clean

Choose the correct word or word pair to complete the following analogies. Then answer the questions.

1. antiseptic : contamination :: _____ : _____

   (a) restraint : movement
   (c) dispensation : absolution

   (b) purifier : respiration
   (d) pedestal: adulation

What relationship sentence did you use to complete this analogy?

2. blameless : culpable :: _____ : cunning

   (a) narcissistic
   (c) guileless
   (e) impervious

   (b) nihilistic
   (d) luckless

110

What relationship sentence did you use to complete this analogy?

What type of analogy is this?

Waiting

Choose the correct word or word pair to complete the following analogies. Below each analogy, write the relationship sentence you used.

1. _____ : wait :: emissary : represent

   (a) descendant   (d) pedant

   (b) ambassador   (e) autocrat

   (c) attendant

2. forbearance : impatient :: _____ : _____

   (a) joyfulness : dour   (d) vindictiveness : proud

   (b) piety: implausible   (e) inquisitiveness : repugnant

   (c) misapprehension : tolerant

111

© 2007 Walch Publishing

Qualities

1. Choose the correct word from the box to complete the following analogy.

| awed   punitive   depraved   emphatic   resilient |

irreverent : _____ :: ethereal : tangible

What relationship sentence did you use to complete this analogy?

2. Choose the correct word pair to complete the following analogy.

parsimonious : money :: _____ : _____

(a) sanctimonious : attitude   (d) hasty : decision

(b) harmonious : nature   (e) terse : speech

(c) guilty : offense

What relationship sentence did you use to solve this analogy?

A Room of One's Own

Choose the correct word or word pair to complete the following analogies. Below each analogy, write the relationship sentence you used.

1. dormitory : slumber :: _____ : _____

   (a) arena : match   (c) moor : zephyr

   (b) empire : despot   (d) embankment : duel

2. ramshackle : structure :: _____ : argument

   (a) persuasive   (d) flimsy

   (b) impenetrable   (e) circular

   (c) insistent

113

Glowing

Choose the correct word or word pair to complete the following analogies. Below each analogy, write the relationship sentence you used.

1. callous : emotional :: _____ : robust

    (a) permissive   (d) vigorous

    (b) infirm   (e) irascible

    (c) deleterious

114

2. glow : luminescent :: _____ : _____

    (a) function : efficient   (c) infer : reminiscent

    (b) evolve : eminent   (d) predict : prescient

Big Ideas

Choose the correct word or word pair to complete the following analogies. Below each analogy, write the relationship sentence you used.

1. fissure : rock :: _____ : ideology

   (a) acknowledgment   (d) dissemination

   (b) understanding   (e) dissention

   (c) schism

2. prehensile : grasp :: _____ : _____

   (a) necessary : invent   (d) fraudulent : employ

   (b) uncomprehending : learn   (e) deciduous : shed

   (c) delirious : enjoy

115

© 2007 Walch Publishing

Take Care

Choose the correct word or word pair to complete the following analogies. Then answer the questions.

1. careful : painstaking :: painful : _____

   (a) excruciating   (d) irritating

   (b) emulating   (e) caretaking

   (c) soothing

What type of analogy is this?

2. prune : tree :: _____ : _____

   (a) flow : river   (c) slash : budget

   (b) incarcerate : felon   (d) handle : suit

What part of speech is *prune* in this analogy?

116

Needling

Choose the correct word pair to complete the following analogies. Then answer the questions.

1. pine : yearn :: _____ : _____

   (a) inhabit : vacate

   (b) facilitate : ease

   (c) fend : welcome

   (d) exacerbate : placate

   (e) transfer : translate

   What part of speech is *pine* in this analogy?

2. _____ : _____ :: teaser : needle

   (a) adherent : stick

   (b) confessor : affirm

   (c) explanation : camouflage

   (d) lesson : instill

   What part of speech is *needle* in this analogy?

117

Causes

Choose the correct word or word pair to complete the following analogies. Then answer the questions.

1. fervent : indifferent :: _____ : _____

    (a) emphatic : unreasonable   (d) alert : determined

    (b) factual : fabricated   (e) sluggish : torpid

    (c) preferable : superior

What relationship sentence did you use to complete this analogy?

2. catalyst : reaction :: _____ : response

    (a) opinion   (b) refusal   (c) infatuation   (d) decimation   (e) trigger

What relationship sentence did you use to complete this analogy?

What type of analogy is this?

Comedy of Errors

Choose the correct word pair to complete the following analogies. Below each analogy, write what type of analogy it is and the relationship sentence you used.

1. farce : drama :: _____ : _____

   (a) music : interlude

   (b) photograph : remnant

   (c) novel : fiction

   (d) canvas : painting

   (e) easel : artist

2. egregious : bad :: _____ : _____

   (a) arrogant : proud

   (b) uncensored : brash

   (c) beleaguered : competent

   (d) disbelieving : suggestible

119

Copycat

Choose the correct word or word pair to complete the following analogies. Below each analogy, write what type of analogy it is and the relationship sentence you used.

1. unique : facsimile :: _____ : enigma

   (a) fastidious   (d) intricate

   (b) uninformed   (e) evasive

   (c) straightforward

2. lynx : feline :: _____ : _____

   (a) nimbus : cloud   (c) apiary : bird

   (b) animal : ranch   (d) wasp : nest

120

Water Works

Choose the correct word or word pair to complete the following analogies. Below each analogy, write the relationship sentence you used.

1. _____ : _____ :: dribble : spew

    (a) enclose : encircle   (d) proclaim : orate

    (b) suggest : urge   (e) excavate : study

    (c) provoke : restrain

2. elastic : pliant :: _____ : doleful

    (a) ecstatic   (d) invincible

    (b) uncertain   (e) imperious

    (c) lugubrious

121

Confidence Game

Choose the correct word pair to complete the following analogies.
Below each analogy, write the relationship sentense you used.

1. undermine : confidence :: _____ : _____

   (a) subsist : ration

   (b) embolden : miscreant

   (c) bolster : opinion

   (d) enable : degradation

   (e) erode : power

2. _____ : _____ :: scam : deceptive

   (a) coin : counterfeit

   (b) affliction : curable

   (c) intellect : malleable

   (d) accident : unintentional

   (e) gorge : unearthed

Daily Warm-Ups: Analogies

122

Home Security

1. Choose the correct word from the box to complete the analogy.

acclimate infuriate jeopardize gesticulate belittle depreciate

minimize : aggrandize :: _____ : secure

What relationship sentence did you use to complete this analogy?

2. Choose the correct word pair to complete the following analogy.

lair : inhabitance :: _____ : _____

   (a) fuel : shortage   (d) dignitary : beneficiary

   (b) merchant : thief   (e) submarine : vessel

   (c) doctrine : maxim

What relationship sentence did you use to complete this analogy?

Move It or Lose It!

Choose the correct word or word pair to complete the following analogies. Then answer the questions.

1. implore : plead :: _____ : lament

   (a) mourn (b) deter (c) beg (d) impugn (e) repudiate

What relationship sentence did you use to complete the analogy?

What type of analogy is this?

124

2. _____ : _____ :: kinetic : motion

   (a) emphatic : speech   (d) incandescent : enthusiasm

   (b) luminescent : sound   (e) capable : effort

   (c) cerebral : intellect

What relationship sentence did you use to solve this analogy?

Happy Anniversary!

Choose the correct word or word pair to complete the following analogies. Below each analogy, write the relationship sentence you used.

1. centennial : anniversary :: _____ : _____

   (a) jubilee : commencement   (c) pilgrimage : explanation

   (b) juncture : forewarning   (d) marathon : race

2. discerning : _____ :: porous : impermeable

   (a) ostentatious   (d) unconcerned

   (b) indiscriminate   (e) enthralled

   (c) impeccable

125

Oops!

Choose the correct word or word pair to complete the following analogies. Then answer the questions.

1. peccadillo : offense :: _____ : _____

   (a) fantasy : reality   (c) peculiarity : tendency

   (b) spat : argument   (d) conviction : punishment

   What relationship sentence did you use to complete this analogy?

   What type of analogy is this?

2. _____ : blunder :: contusion : bruise

   (a) gaffe   (d) volition

   (b) confection   (e) enumeration

   (c) implosion

   What relationship sentence did you use to complete this analogy?

126

A Little Knowledge

Choose the correct word or word pair to complete the following analogies. Below each analogy, write the relationship sentence you used.

1. obscure : fact :: _____ : knowledge

   (a) unbelievable   (d) esoteric

   (b) common   (e) vitriolic

   (c) imperiled

2. logic : cogent :: _____ : _____

   (a) bonus : unearned   (d) circumspection : unavoidable

   (b) chronology : inaccurate (e) cacophony : atonal

   (c) inclination : malevolent

127

Choices

Choose the correct word or word pair to complete the following analogies. Below each analogy, write the relationship sentence you used.

1. indecisive : choose :: unyielding : _____

   (a) insist

   (b) select

   (c) compromise

   (d) contain

   (e) deter

128

2. dilemma : choice :: _____ : _____

   (a) conundrum : problem

   (b) tragedy : comedy

   (c) facsimile : original

   (d) wit : wisdom

   (e) fidelity : virtue

Don't Be Angry

Choose the correct word from the box to complete the following analogies.

| lithe   migratory   fierce   smoldering   livid |

1. ferocious : _____ :: ardent : impassioned

2. mandatory : voluntary :: settled : _____

3. careful : meticulous :: angry : _____

4. contortionist : _____ :: savant : knowledgeable

5. _____ : ember :: vestigial : trace

129

Pride and Prejudice

Choose the correct word or word pair to complete the following analogies. Below each analogy, write what type of analogy it is and the relationship sentence you used.

1. proud : haughty :: _____ : forbidding

   (a) awesome   (d) inviting

   (b) imposing   (e) menacing

   (c) revealing

2. _____ : _____ :: predilection : distaste

   (a) enclosure : embankment   (c) tremor : impatience

   (b) insolence : respect   (d) inconclusiveness : hesitancy

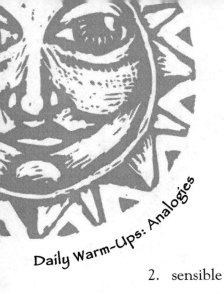

Sense and Sensibility

Choose the correct word or word pair to complete the following analogies. Below each analogy, write the relationship sentence you used.

1. sense : aware :: _____ : _____

   (a) ignore : infantile   (c) investigate : determined

   (b) attack : docile   (d) understand : astute

2. sensible : perceive :: _____ : understand

   (a) impeccable   (d) satiable

   (b) credible   (e) fanciful

   (c) knowable

131

Persuasion

Choose the correct word or word pair to complete the following analogies. Below each analogy, write the relationship sentence you used.

1. wheedle : cajole :: _____ : cause

   (a) indicate

   (b) effect

   (c) deduce

   (d) vow

   (e) precipitate

132

2. _____ : _____ :: sway : opinion

   (a) believe : abstraction

   (b) switch : allegiance

   (c) defeat : opponent

   (d) subdue : belligerence

Heroes and Villains

Choose the correct word or word pair to complete the following analogies. Below each analogy, write what type of analogy it is and the relationship sentence you used.

1. nefarious : malefactor :: _____ : _____

   (a) devious : intruder

   (b) deranged : resistor

   (c) disingenuous : prevaricator

   (d) overbearing : malcontent

   (e) insidious : tenant

2. champion : advocate :: overseer : _____

   (a) envision

   (b) repudiate

   (c) deny

   (d) supervise

Happiness

Choose the correct word or word pair to complete the following analogies. Below each analogy, write the relationship sentence you used.

1. exhilarated : gleeful :: _____ : _____

   (a) frantic : nervous

   (b) correct : unerring

   (c) disbelieving : credulous

   (d) depressed : exhausted

   (e) exasperated : irked

2. _____ : sorrow :: jubilation : joy

   (a) orientation

   (b) lamentation

   (c) celebration

   (d) pigmentation

   (e) emancipation

134

Daily Warm-Ups: Analogies

Power

Choose the correct word or word pair to complete the following analogies. Below each analogy, write the relationship sentence you used.

1. magnate : power :: _____ : _____

   (a) engineer : efficiency

   (b) oaf : catastrophe

   (c) despot : diplomacy

   (d) eulogist : sympathy

   (e) juvenile : youth

2. circuitous : route :: _____ : behavior

   (a) alarming

   (b) evasive

   (c) empowering

   (d) unwavering

Characteristics

Choose the correct word or word pair to complete the following analogies. Below each analogy, write the relationship sentence you used.

1. teacher : didactic :: improviser : _____

   (a) untrained   (d) inquisitive

   (b) extemporaneous   (e) demanding

   (c) fastidious

2. dilettante : focus :: _____ : _____

   (a) spendthrift : greed   (c) informant : information

   (b) plagiarist : opulence   (d) pariah : acceptance

Decoration

Choose the correct word or word pair to complete the following analogies. Below each analogy, write what type of analogy it is and the relationship sentence you used.

1. garland : festoon :: _____ : _____

    (a) domicile : relocate   (d) elixir : entertain

    (b) effigy : release   (e) cable : disconnect

    (c) leash : tether

2. rococo : ornate :: _____ : questionable

    (a) dubious   (d) cautious

    (b) curious   (e) absolute

    (c) precarious

137

Home Sweet Home

Choose the correct word or word pair to complete the following analogies. Below each analogy, write what type of analogy it is and the relationship sentence you used.

1. yurt : dwelling :: _____ : _____

    (a) cello : instrument   (c) smile : grimace

    (b) highway : vehicle   (d) buttress : building

2. _____ : empathetic :: domesticated : feral

    (a) compassionate   (c) undeserving   (e) indifferent

    (b) bewildered   (d) obsequious

138

Daily Warm-Ups: Analogies

Law and Order

Choose the correct word or word pair to complete the following analogies. Below each analogy, write the relationship sentence you used.

1. police : precinct :: _____ : _____

   (a) teacher : curriculum

   (b) judge : jurisdiction

   (c) athlete : competition

   (d) manager : leadership

   (e) captain : ocean

2. methodical : imprecision :: _____ : compatibility

   (a) deranged

   (b) impassive

   (c) comely

   (d) punctual

   (e) unsuited

139

So Many Questions

Choose the correct word or word pair to complete the following analogies. Below each analogy, write the relationship sentence you used.

1. _____ : consciousness :: inquiry : query

   (a) concoction

   (b) conspicuousness

   (c) convalescence

   (d) cognizance

   (e) constancy

140

2. opaque : translucence :: _____ : _____

   (a) serious : frivolity

   (b) compromised : impairment

   (c) incapable : promise

   (d) inarguable : logic

   (e) consequential : news

Pandemonium

Choose the correct word or word pair to complete the following analogies. Then answer the questions.

1. emollient : soften :: panacea : _____

    (a) soothe (b) embroil (c) cure (d) recede

What relationship sentence did you use to complete this analogy?

What type of analogy is this?

2. panoramic : view :: _____ : _____

    (a) surly : disposition   (d) effacing : self

    (b) comprehensive : understanding   (e) tentative : plan

    (c) spurious : reasoning

What relationship sentence did you use to complete this analogy?

141

Declarations

Choose the correct word or word pair to complete the following analogies. Below each analogy, write the relationship sentence you used.

1. _____ : declare :: stupefy : astound

   (a) profess   (c) shock   (e) maraud

   (b) deter   (d) deny

142

2. independent : shackled :: _____ : _____

   (a) gloomy : melancholy   (c) manipulative : tolerable

   (b) spirited : lethargic   (d) lurid : grizzly

Demanding

1. Choose the correct word from the box to complete the following analogy.

| idiosyncratic | idyllic | impertinent | implacable | impalpable |

importunate : demanding :: _____ : eccentric

What relationship sentence did you use to solve this analogy?

2. Choose the correct word pair to complete the following analogy.

eager : rapacious :: _____ : _____

(a) helpful : detrimental

(b) extraneous : crucial

(c) needy : destitute

(d) informative : dull

(e) incendiary : provoking

What relationship sentence did you use to complete this analogy?

143

© 2007 Walch Publishing

Fighting Words

Choose the correct word or word pair to complete the following analogies. Below each analogy, write what type of analogy it is and the relationship sentence you used.

1. pugilist : fight :: hedonist : _____

   (a) injure   (d) imagine

   (b) enjoin   (e) ingratiate

   (c) indulge

2. bellicose : peaceable :: _____ : _____

   (a) flawed : impeccable   (d) reticent : shy

   (b) irreversible : unadvisable   (e) tedious : paralyzing

   (c) inadvertent : unintentional

Catch

Choose the correct word or word pair to complete the following analogies. Below each analogy, write what type of analogy it is and the relationship sentence you used.

1. captor : encage :: _____ : _____

   (a) victor : capitulate   (c) charlatan : endeavor

   (b) recidivist : improve   (d) faultfinder : cavil

2. trap : ensnare :: kindling : _____

   (a) ignite   (c) encompass   (e) apprehend

   (b) engulf   (d) recede

145

© 2007 Walch Publishing

Unwell

Choose the correct word or word pair to complete the following analogies. Below each analogy, write the relationship sentence you used.

1. _____ : _____ :: torpid : sluggish

   (a) anemic : sanguine   (d) enfeebled : virulent

   (b) tremulous : steady   (e) wan : pale

   (c) febrile : delirious

2. inoculation : immunity :: _____ : response

   (a) observation   (d) conclusion

   (b) prompt   (e) datum

   (c) hypothesis

Boastful

Choose the correct word or word pair to complete the following analogies. Below each analogy, write the relationship sentence you used.

1. _____ : _____ :: braggart : humility

    (a) troglodyte : oafishness   (d) ignoramus : understanding

    (b) harbinger : compassion   (e) emissary : purpose

    (c) commentator : loquaciousness

2. assurance : conceited :: shyness : _____

    (a) malleable   (d) enviable

    (b) risible   (e) diffident

    (c) docile

Daily Warm-Ups: Analogies

147

© 2007 Walch Publishing

Vocal Chords

Choose the correct word or word pair to complete the following analogies. Below each analogy, write what type of analogy it is and the relationship sentence you used.

1. mellifluous : grating :: _____ : _____

   (a) humorless : facetious
   (c) courageous : inquisitive
   (b) lachrymose : tearful
   (d) independent : dissipated

2. traitor : treason :: liar : _____

   (a) penury
   (d) posterity
   (b) prosperity
   (e) perpetuation
   (c) perjury

148

Going Bald

Choose the correct word or word pair to complete the following analogies. Below each analogy, write the relationship sentence you used.

1. hirsute : hairless :: _____ : _____

    (a) inopportune : fortunate   (d) capable : inept

    (b) endearing : loveable   (e) ecstatic : pleased

    (c) savvy : sophisticated

2. recede : tide :: _____ : moon

    (a) shine   (c) wax   (e) revolve

    (b) wane   (d) waver

Long Time

Choose the correct word to complete the following analogies.
Below each analogy, write the relationship sentence you used.

1. unequivocal : _____ :: ephemeral : longevity

   (a) equidistant   (d) unassuming

   (b) average   (e) ambiguous

   (c) determined

2. stamina : endurance :: _____ : wit

   (a) jocularity   (d) wisdom

   (b) sobriety   (e) judiciousness

   (c) determination

150

Dense

Choose the correct word to complete the following analogies.
Then answer the questions.

1. _____ : liquid :: dense : fog

   (a) dilute   (c) viscous   (e) evaporated

   (b) brackish   (d) potable

What relationship sentense did you use to complete this analogy?

2. sparse : barren :: torn : _____

(a) mended (b) lacerated (c) impaired (d) certain (e) negligible

What relationship sentence did you use to complete this analogy?

What type of analogy is this?

Daily Warm-Ups: Analogies

151

Beginnings

Choose the correct word or word pair to complete the following analogies. Below each analogy, write what type of analogy it is and the relationship sentence you used.

1. begin : initiator :: _____ : emulator

   (a) relish   (c) attempt   (e) adhere

   (b) ensue   (d) ape

152

2. inauguration : ceremony :: _____ : _____

   (a) commentary : complaint   (c) affidavit : statement

   (b) citadel : welcome   (d) partition : opening

City Life

Choose the correct word or word pair to complete the following analogies. Then answer the questions.

1. bucolic : city :: _____ : _____

    (a) orderly : riot   (d) rural : pasture

    (b) provoked : strife   (e) gracious : manner

    (c) calculated : action

Even if you didn't know what bucolic meant, were there any answer choices you could rule out because of a weak relationship between the words?

2. architect : design :: correspondent : _____

    (a) ensue   (b) enhance   (c) relate   (d) deviate   (e) efface

Which type of analogy is this?

© 2007 Walch Publishing

Rare Ribs

Choose the correct word or word pair to complete the following analogies. Then answer the questions.

1. rarity : ubiquitous :: truism : _____

   (a) logical   (c) invaluable

   (b) credible   (d) debatable

What relationship sentence did you use to complete this analogy?

2. _____ : _____ :: rib : ridicule

   (a) comprehend : decry   (d) enable : halt

   (b) encourage : force   (e) fortify : weaken

   (c) entail : curtail

What relationship sentence did you use to complete this analogy?

What type of analogy is this?

154

Guilty Party

1. Choose the correct word from the box to complete the following analogy.

unparalleled culpable ingenious imprisoned enraged

   indigenous : native :: _____ : perpetrator

   What type of analogy is this?

2. Choose the correct word pair to complete the following analogy.

   gala : festive :: _____ : _____

   (a) benefit : productive   (c) accusation : false

   (b) affront : determined   (d) platitude : trite

   What type of analogy is this?

155

© 2007 Walch Publishing

Repent!

Choose the correct word or word pair to complete the following analogies. Below each analogy, write the relationship sentence you used.

1. repentant : contrition :: _____ : _____

    (a) indulgent : penitence

    (b) curious: knowledge

    (c) eclectic : resistance

    (d) impervious : sensitivity

    (e) gregarious : conviviality

2. sympathetic : _____ :: rueful : regret

    (a) sorrow

    (b) hope

    (c) compassion

    (d) embarrassment

    (e) heartlessness

Cowardice

Choose the correct word pair to complete the following analogies. Below each analogy, write what type of analogy it is and the relationship sentence you used.

1. craven : coward :: _____ : _____

   (a) disbelieving : maverick

   (b) jaded : cynic

   (c) caustic : skeptic

   (d) peripheral : contributor

   (e) honest : charlatan

2. _____ : _____ :: tremor : quake

   (a) drizzle : deluge

   (b) flake : flurry

   (c) attack : retreat

   (d) canyon : plateau

Rise Up

Choose the correct word or word pair to complete the following analogies. Below each analogy, write the relationship sentence you used.

1. sedition : rebellion :: _____ : deceit

   (a) earnestness   (d) chicanery

   (b) clarity   (e) hedonism

   (c) hyperbole

2. ascension : decline :: _____ : _____

   (a) cautiousness : timidity   (d) inducement : scheme

   (b) increase : escalation   (e) periphery : summit

   (c) elevation : depression

158

Clean Up the Streets

Choose the correct word or word pair to complete the following analogies. Below each analogy, write what type of analogy it is and the relationship sentence you used.

1. antiseptic : sterilize :: _____ : _____

   (a) adhesive : stick   (c) decontaminant : waste

   (b) radiator : enmesh   (d) aspirator : exhale

2. criminal : felonious :: imposter : _____

   (a) improper   (d) enriched

   (b) besieged   (e) befuddled

   (c) fraudulent

159

Heavy

Choose the correct word to complete the following analogies. Below each analogy, write what type of analogy it is and the relationship sentence you used.

1. _____ : hinder :: barricade : block

   (a) projectile   (c) salutation

   (b) interpretation   (d) encumbrance

2. portentous : weighty :: _____ : light

   (a) unappealing   (c) shadowy   (e) frivolous

   (b) blinding   (d) stoic

Don't Think Twice

Choose the correct word or word pair to complete the following analogies. Below each analogy, write the relationship sentence you used.

1. alacrity : hesitation :: prosperity : _____

   (a) munificence   (d) insolvency

   (b) generosity   (e) expediency

   (c) misfortune

2. pensive : mull :: _____ : _____

   (a) intrusive : deflect   (d) restive : nap

   (b) evasive : lie   (e) passive : act

   (c) abrasive : irritate

161

It's All Right

Choose the correct word or word pair to complete the following analogies. Below each analogy, write what type of analogy it is and the relationship sentence you used.

1. accord : disagreement :: _____ : _____

   (a) profusion : scarcity

   (c) immediacy : proximity

   (b) tenet : principle

   (d) shock : disdain

Daily Warm-Ups: Analogies

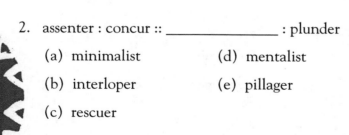

162

2. assenter : concur :: _____ : plunder

   (a) minimalist

   (d) mentalist

   (b) interloper

   (e) pillager

   (c) rescuer

Beware

Choose the correct word or word pair to complete the following analogies. Then answer the questions.

1. risky : perilous :: _____ : _____

    (a) malodorous : pleasant

    (d) exuberant : terrified

    (b) believing : adamant

    (e) protruding : protracted

    (c) lofty : hopeful

What relationship sentence did you use to complete this analogy?

What type of analogy is this?

2. inclement : weather :: _____ : mood

    (a) brightening

    (c) incandescent

    (e) foul

    (b) unwavering

    (d) unreadable

What relationship sentence did you use to complete this analogy?

© 2007 Walch Publishing

High Achiever

Choose the correct word or word pair to complete the following analogies. Below each analogy, write the relationship sentence you used.

1. illustrious : eminence :: _____ : productivity

   (a) industrious   (d) unsustainable

   (b) elusive   (e) trainable

   (c) unattainable

164

2. master : accomplished :: _____ : _____

   (a) deceiver : honest   (d) victor : impartial

   (b) swindler : impure   (e) professor : intemperate

   (c) sovereign : authoritative

Running Short

Choose the correct word or word pair to complete the following analogies. Then answer the questions.

1. delivery : courier :: _____ : _____

   (a) instigation : inspector
   (d) incrimination : journalist

   (b) condemnation : jury
   (e) representation : agent

   (c) resuscitation : doctor

What relationship sentence did you use to complete this analogy?

What type of analogy is this?

2. truncate : limb :: _____ : conversation

   (a) initiate
   (c) repeat
   (e) internalize

   (b) curtail
   (d) vocalize

What relationship sentence did you use to complete this analogy?

165

© 2007 Walch Publishing

Might Makes Right

Choose the correct word or word pair to complete the following analogies. Below each analogy, write the relationship sentence you used.

1. deliberation : _____ :: might : frailty

   (a) spontaneity

   (b) impetuousness

   (c) generosity

   (d) luminescence

   (e) carelessness

2. infringe : right :: _____ : _____

   (a) meddle : argument

   (b) interfere : attempt

   (c) trespass : property

   (d) alleviate : pain

166

Maybe, Maybe Not

Choose the correct word pair to complete the following analogies. Below each analogy, write the relationship sentence you used.

1. _____ : _____ :: ambivalence : contradiction

   (a) insistence : righteousness   (c) hyperbole : excess

   (b) deliberation : hurriedness   (d) defiance : dependence

2. manifesto : declaration :: _____ : _____

   (a) insignia : uniform   (d) disbelief : paranoia

   (b) utterance : language   (e) wave : gesture

   (c) interaction : negligence

167

Eat and Be Merry

Choose the correct word or word pair to complete the following analogies. Then answer the questions.

1. banquet : meal :: _____ : _____

   (a) iconoclast : tradition   (c) embellishment : story

   (b) vestment : decoration   (d) palace : house

What relationship sentence did you use to complete this analogy?

What type of analogy is this?

168

2. _____ : merriment :: apex : nadir

   (a) excitement   (b) cheer   (c) gloom   (d) incitement   (e) incongruity

What relationship sentence did you use to complete this analogy?

Simplify

Choose the correct word or word pair to complete the following analogies. Below each analogy, write what type of analogy it is and the relationship sentence you used.

1. condense : reduction :: filter : _____

   (a) dehydration   (d) continuation

   (b) purification   (e) cauterization

   (c) infiltration

2. cacophony : discordant :: _____ : _____

   (a) abstraction : meaningful   (c) abyss : hopeful

   (b) melee : chaotic   (d) leader : charismatic

169

In a Bubble

Choose the correct word or word pair to complete the following analogies. Below each analogy, write the relationship sentence you used.

1. ebullient : effervescent :: _____ : fractious

   (a) recalcitrant   (d) claustrophobic

   (b) abbreviated   (e) aristocratic

   (c) nonchalant

2. _____ : _____ :: oblivious : awareness

   (a) introspective : perspective   (c) patient : reluctance

   (b) decisive : uncertainty   (d) impassioned : interest

Sound Off

Choose the correct word or word pair to complete the following analogies. Below each analogy, write what type of analogy it is and the relationship sentence you used.

1. _____ : _____ :: din : noise

   (a) neon : color   (c) spice : flavor

   (b) optician : vision   (d) stench : smell

Daily Warm-Ups: Analogies

2. sycophant : _____ :: proselytizer : convert

   (a) dismiss   (c) vend   (e) flatter

   (b) heal   (d) rupture

171

Improvements

Choose the correct word or word pair to complete the following analogies. Below each analogy, write the relationship sentence you used.

1. quench : thirst :: _____ : grief

   (a) prolong   (c) inflict   (e) assuage

   (b) ensue   (d) adorn

Daily Warm-Ups: Analogies

172

2. mitigation : exacerbate :: _____ : _____

   (a) indignation : tolerate   (d) communication : expedite

   (b) gentrification : elaborate   (e) conflagration : emulate

   (c) elongation : abbreviate

Common Cause

Choose the correct word or word pair to complete the following analogies. Then answer the questions.

1. plebian : pedestrian :: unyielding : _____

    (a) resolute

    (d) parsimonious

    (b) infirm

    (e) illustrious

    (c) industrious

    What part of speech is *pedestrian*?

2. _____ : _____ :: instigator : provoke

    (a) scholar : insinuate

    (c) calculator : calibrate

    (b) investor : depreciate

    (d) mediator : intervene

    What type of analogy is this?

173

© 2007 Walch Publishing

Past Perfect

Choose the correct word or word pair to complete the following analogies. Below each analogy, write the relationship sentence you used.

1. archaic : modern :: _____ : _____

   (a) extemporaneous : spontaneous (c) prohibited : permitted

   (b) creative : original   (d) dethroned : ironic

174

2. _____ : perfection :: labyrinth : intricacy

   (a) pandemic   (d) attainment

   (b) utopia   (e) aspiration

   (c) befuddlement

Tasty

Choose the correct word or word pair to complete the following analogies. Below each analogy, write what type of analogy it is and the relationship sentence you used.

1. pepper : spice :: _____ : _____

   (a) chicken : bird   (c) seed : stem

   (b) root : tree   (d) vegetable : mineral

2. confection : sweet :: desert : _____

   (a) caloric   (d) indulgent

   (b) expansive   (e) arid

   (c) unknowable

175

Forbidden Fruit

Choose the correct word or word pair to complete the following analogies. Below each analogy, write the relationship sentence you used.

1. _____ : trade :: ban : goods

   (a) treaty   (d) contingency

   (b) summit   (e) embargo

   (c) conference

2. culinary : food :: _____ : _____

   (a) arbitrary : decision   (c) territorial : expansion

   (b) terrestrial : earth   (d) monetary : transaction

176

All Wrong

Choose the correct word or word pair to complete the following analogies. Below each analogy, write the relationship sentence you used.

1. fallacy : erroneous :: _____ : _____

    (a) understanding : optional   (c) opinion : informed

    (b) privation : luxurious   (d) necessity : essential

Daily Warm-Ups: Analogies

2. err : mistake :: _____ : speculation

    (a) infer   (c) conjecture   (e) deliberate

    (b) recreate   (d) earn

177

Bad Deal

Choose the correct word or word pair to complete the following analogies. Below each analogy, write what type of analogy it is and the relationship sentence you used.

1. fleece : swindle :: postpone : _____

   (a) defer   (c) declare   (e) hasten

   (b) stake   (d) conclude

2. _____ : _____ :: mishap : catastrophe

   (a) surprise : shock   (c) allegiance : enemy

   (b) embellishment : ornamentation   (d) friendship : amity

178

Expensive

Choose the correct word or word pair to complete the following analogies. Below each analogy, write what type of analogy it is and the relationship sentence you used.

1. gratuitous : costly :: _____ : objective

   (a) achievable   (d) selective

   (b) intolerable   (e) subjective

   (c) defective

2. exorbitant : expensive :: _____ : _____

   (a) incurious : intelligent   (c) unmoved : emotional

   (b) outlandish : odd   (d) disdainful : empathetic

So Long

Choose the correct word or word pair to complete the following analogies. Below each analogy, write the relationship sentence you used.

1. ultimate : initial :: _____ : forced

   (a) unequivocal   (d) elusive

   (b) obtrusive   (e) impressive

   (c) spontaneous

2. meandering : road :: _____ : _____

   (a) circuitous : argument   (d) discernible : vision

   (b) opinionated : speaker   (e) impeccable : garment

   (c) articulated : sound

1. *Cowardly* is the opposite of *courageous*; b
2. *Digit* is to *finger* as *limb* is to *arm*; d
3. The function of *teeth* is to *chew*; d
4. a, c; A group of *ships* make up a *fleet*; c
5. e
6. instrument
7. Suggested answer: decide, instruct, portray; d
8. To *transport* is the function of a *vehicle*; connect
9. A *ripple* is a small *wave*. To be extremely *thin* is to be *emaciated*. To *race* is to go much faster than to *saunter*; a
10. A *performer* is found in a *theater*; A *theater* is where a *performer* is found; a
11. To *impede* is to create an *obstacle*; Something will *begin* after it is *instigated*; b
12. An *archipelago* is a group of *islands*; c
13. serpent; e
14. Sample answer: dry; embellished; uproar; c
15. Sample answer: strength; lack; unbelievable; sparse
16. d
17. An *oracle* can *foresee* the future; An *oracle* makes a *prediction*; a

18. adulation; Something *laudable* deserves *adulation*. To give *encouragement* is the opposite of *deride*.
19. 1. c; *Loquacious* describes very wordy *speech*.
    2. e; A *monologue* is a performance given by a single *actor*. Students might have had to adjust sentence to include "single," to exclude choice (b).
20. 1. c; agent : action
    2. deteriorate; To lose *value* is to *depreciate*.
21. 1. e; To *abhor* is to strongly *dislike*; action : lesser degree
    2. liberate; To *inculpate* is to *blame*; word : synonym
22. 1. *Secretive* means keeping secrets; *Candor* means openness; Someone who is *secretive* lacks *candor*; a
    2. c; agent : action (in reverse order)
23. 1. a; description: greater degree; Something *bitter* is extremely *acrid*.
    2. time; *Gustatory* means having to do with *taste*.
24. 1. c; person : description; A *glutton* is someone who *indulges*.
    2. d; Something without *limit* is *infinite*.

Daily Warm-Ups: Analogies

5. 1. d; c; Something *somnolent* causes *sleep*.
2. a; word : antonym

26. 1. b; person : description (reverse order)
2. c; a *weaver* creates a *tapestry*

27. 1. a; a *squall* is a sudden *storm*; object : category
2. gale; object : greater degree

28. 1. b; noun; noun; word : antonym
2. c; to *treasure* a *memory* is to greatly appreciate it

29. 1. static; *Exhilarated* is the opposite of *depressed*.
2. e; a and b

30. 1. a; cause : effect
2. b; A *general* is the head of an *army*; a and d

31. The function of a *shelf* is *storage*; object : function
Suggested answers: shelter, division, detergent

32. 1. hesitate; word : synonym
2. c; word : antonym

33. 1. d; The job of a *potentate* is to *rule*.
2. b; *Seclusion* is the habit of a *recluse*.

34. 1. e; pale; Something *wan* lacks *color*.
2. a; *Flimsy* describes *fabric* that lacks substance.

35. 1. d; Someone *selfless* lacks *greed*.
2. a; word : synonym; Choices c and d both contain word pairs with no clear relationship, so you can eliminate them right away.

36. 1. c; word : antonym
2. boon; word : antonym; Answers will vary.

37. 1. e; person : description
2. b; agent : action; The action of a *speaker* is to *orate*.

38. 1. b; *Deliberate* is the opposite of *accidental*.
2. a; d and e are common words that have nothing to do with *gravity*; Something *deceptive* is characterized by *trickery*.

39. 1. c; description : greater degree
2. c; To *repent* is to be *remorseful*.

40. 1. a; verb; the corresponding words are all verbs; word : antonym
2. d; To *erode* is to eat away at *land*.

41. 1. c; *Grazing* takes place in a *pasture*.
2. cast; A group of *musicians* is an *ensemble*; *soliloquy* and *monologue*

42. 1. b; To *penetrate* something is to get to its *core*.
2. e; A *footnote* comes at the end of a *chapter*; answers will vary.

43. 1. c; word : synonym
2. d; word : antonym

Daily Warm-Ups: Analogies

3. a; cause : effect

4. b; part : whole

44. 1. c; *Obtuse* is the opposite of *sharp*.

2. a; No—vision may or may not be acute, so it's not object : description; *Acute* describes sharp *vision*.

45. 1. b; *Peek* is a lesser degree of *ogle*.

2. e; word : synonym

46. 1. b; yes; agent : action; An *assailant*, by definition, *attacks*.

2. detailed; *Corpulent* is the opposite of *lithe*.

47. 1. d; someone who resists war or promotes peace; A *pacifist* opposes *fighting*.

2. d; whole : part; A piece of *pie* is called a *wedge*.

48. 1. a; Answers will vary—perhaps b and c; To *slake* is to cure *thirst*.

2. c; b and d are both word : antonyms, so both can be eliminated

49. 1. e; To *obfuscate* is to create *confusion*.

2. a; *Foreboding* is the expectation of *misfortune*.

50. 1. d; A *caper* is an *adventure*.

2. a; Individual *cattle* make up a *herd*.

3. b; To *dabble* is a lesser degree of *delve*.

4. c; An *orator* stands at a *podium*.

51. 1. c; word : synonym; Answers will vary.

2. Suggested answers: respect, honor; verb; To *ruminate* is to *ponder*.

52. 1. d; *Tactile* means related to *touch*; Answers will vary.

2. b; *Tenuous* describes a *weak* grasp.

53. 1. c; *Succinct* is the opposite of *verbose*; b and d

2. b; *Direction* is measured by a *compass*.

54. 1. a; cause-effect; To *incite* is to start a *riot*.

2. e; action : greater degree

55. 1. d; *Shoplifting* is a type of *theft*.

2. e; part : whole (reversed); A *band* is a group of *pirates*.

56. 1. praise : belittle (or other way around); word : antonym

2. e; A group of *words* makes up a *sentence*; Answers will vary.

57. 1. b; A *scapegoat* is someone people *blame*.

2. c; agent : action

58. 1. a; *Saccharine* means extremely *sweet*.

2. d; agent : action; The job of a *censor* is to *delete*.

59. 1. a; To *launch* an *investigation* is to start it.

Daily Warm-Ups: Analogies

2. torment : tease; action : lesser degree

60. 1. d; A *neophyte* by definition is not *seasoned*.
    2. b; *Verdant* is a synonym for *lush*.
61. 1. c, 2. b, 3. e, 4. d, 5. a, 6. f, 7. h, 8. g
62. 1. c; A *paradox* is, by definition, *contradictory*;
    object : description
    2. a; word : antonym
63. 1. b; *Sleet* is a type of *precipitation*.
    2. clashing; no; *Discordant tones* don't go well
    together.
64. 1. c; *Temerity* is the opposite to the characteristic of
    a *coward*.
    2. a; A *statement* that is *baseless* has no substance.
65. 1. d; yes; object : function (reversed); To *adhere* is
    the function of *glue*.
    2. b; word : synonym; A *sycophant* is the same as
    a *toady*.
66. 1. b; *Antebellum* means the time before a *war*.
    2. a; action : greater degree
67. 1. c; The function of *water* is to *hydrate*; object :
    function (reversed)
    2. e; word : synonym; Answers will vary.
68. 1. d; To be *candid* is to *reveal*.

2. c; *Refined* is the opposite of *boorish*;
   word : antonym
69. 1. b; *Miserly* describes the opposite of a *benefactor*.
    2. adherents; A *clan* is made up of *members*;
    Answers will vary. Students might have had to
    revise from "A *clan* contains *members*," as that
    would not rule out the other answers.
70. 1. b; To *inculpate* is the opposite action as
    exoneration.
    2. a; A *naïf*, by definition, is the opposite of *jaded*.
71. 1. d; *Birds* are kept in an *aviary*; object : location
    2. c; An *aviator* conducts a *flight*; agent : action
72. 1. a; *Agoraphobia* is a type of *fear*; object : category
    2. c; *Juvenescence* is the opposite of *age*.
73. 1. c; To *pilfer goods* is to *steal* them.
    2. e; To *thwart* is to *frustrate*; word : synonym
74. 1. flammable; An *irascible temper* ignites easily.
    2. c; *Incendiary* is the same as *flammable*; word :
    synonym
75. 1. b; A *fable* is a type of *tale*; object : category
    2. b; Someone *credulous* is characterized by
    gullibility.
76. 1. a; To *clarify* is to eliminate *confusion*.

2. e; An *ascetic* is characterized by *austerity*; person : description

77. 1. d; Something *intangible* cannot be *touched*.
2. b; Something *affecting* causes a *response*; cause : effect

78. 1. preserve; The action of a *pugilist* is to *fight*; agent : action
2. c; *Disputants* lack *accord*; d and e

79. 1. a; A serial is made up of installments; part : whole (reversed)
2. d; An *intricate pattern* is highly detailed.

80. 1. e; A *coward*, by definition, is not *intrepid*.
2. b; action : greater degree

81. 1. b; A *glutton* is characterized by *excess*; person : description
2. a; The function of a *knife* is to *incise*; object : function

82. 1. d; Someone who is *animated* lacks *lethargy*.
2. a; *Vim* is the same as *energy*; word : synonym

83. 1. c; *Somnolent* is the opposite of *invigorating*.
2. b; The function of an *awl* is to *bore*; object : function

84. 1. c; An *imbroglio* is a very large *tiff*; object : lesser degree

85. 1. corrode; To *erode* is to wear away *land*.
2. e; *Saline*, by definition, describes *brine*; object : description (reversed)

86. 1. b; To *satiate* is to satisfy an *appetite*.
2. d; *Edible* describes *fare* that can be consumed.

87. 1. a; *Chaos* is the same as *pandemonium*.
2. e; A *chronology* is a list of *events*.

88. 1. c; A *miser* is not *munificent*.
2. d; A *philanthropist* is the same as a *benefactor*.

89. 1. b; An *inchoate opinion* is vague.
2. conviction; word : antonym

90. 1. c; *Dexterous* means nimble with the *hands*.
2. b; *Surprised* is a lesser degree of *stunned*.
3. e; A *spark* causes something to *ignite*.
4. a; *Impede* is the opposite of *facilitate*.
5. d; *Paucity* is the opposite of *dearth*.

91. Answers will vary. Sample answers:
1. stingy
2. player
3. frenetic
4. demanding

5. fetid

92. 1. a; To *expunge* is to remove from *memory*.
    2. d; *Discriminating* describes an *epicure*; person: description (reversed)

93. 1. e; The function of a *buoy* is to *float*; object : function
    2. d; *Familiar* is the opposite of *exotic*; word : antonym

94. 1. a; To *cajole* is to *wheedle*.
    2. c; A *virtuoso* is defined by *talent*; person : description

95. 1. b; *Apex* is the opposite of *nadir*.
    2. c; A *mesa* is a type of *formation*; object : category

96. 1. b; A *prolific writer* produces a lot.
    2. d; *Procrastination* is the action of a *shirker*; agent : action (reversed)

97. 1. d; To *decorate* is the purpose of an *adornment*; object : function (reversed)
    2. e; To *raze* a *building* is to completely destroy it.

98. 1. recall; To *recant* an *opinion* is to take it back.
    2. c; To *opine* is to state a *belief*.

99. 1. b; A *tenuous* describes a *hold* that isn't strong.
    2. a; A *jester* is the same as a *prankster*.

100. 1. d; A *curmudgeon* is, by definition, *disgruntled*; yes; person : description
     2. e; *Glum* is a lesser degree of *despondent*; description : greater degree

101. 1. b; A *theologian* studies *religion*; answers will vary.
     2. a; *Embezzlement* is the stealing of *funds*.

102. 1. c; *Sloth* is the same as *torpidity*; word : synonym
     2. d; *Mortal* describes a *wound* that is deadly.

103. 1. e; A *pamphlet* is a much smaller version of a *tome*; object: greater size
     2. b; A *bibliophile* loves *books*; agent : object

104. Answers will vary. Sample answers:
     1. frivolous; *Sporadic* is the opposite of *predictable*.
     2. uncaring; *Vehement* is the same as *fervent*.
     3. rule; A *vagrant* by definition *wanders*.
     4. miserly; *Confident* as a lesser degree of *brazen*.
     5. spend; *Inter* is the opposite of *unearth*.

105. 1. d; To *repeal* a *law* is to take it back.
     2. a; *Saucy* is the same as *impudent*; word : synonym

106. c; The job of a *delegate* is to provide *representation*; agent : action; noun

107. 1. b; A *serpentine river* winds around.
     2. a; An *asp* is a type of *snake*; object : category

108. 1. c; *Bovine* means relating to or resembling a *cow*.
     2. d; *Pedigree* is a synonym for *lineage*.
109. 1. e; *Concentrated* is the opposite of *dilute*; adjective
     2. b; *Glance* is a lesser degree of *pore*.
110. 1. a; An *antiseptic* prevents *contamination*.
     2. c; Someone *blameless* is not *culpable*; person : description
111. 1. c; The job of an *emissary* is to *represent*.
     2. a; Somebody with *forbearance* is not *impatient*.
112. 1. awed; *Ethereal* means the opposite of *tangible*.
     2. e; *Parsimonious* means frugal with *money*.
113. 1. a; A *dormitory* is a place for *slumber*.
     2. d; A *ramshackle structure* is poorly constructed.
114. 1. b; *Callous* is the opposite of *emotional*.
     2. d; Something that *glows* is *luminescent*.
115. 1. c; A *fissure* is a split in a *rock*.
     2. e; Something *prehensile grasps*.
116. 1. a; action : greater degree
     2. c; verb
117. 1. b; verb
     2. a; verb
118. 1. b; *Fervent* is the opposite of *indifferent*.
     2. e; A *catalyst* starts a *reaction*; cause : effect

119. 1. c; A *farce* is a type of *drama*; object : category
     2. a; *Egregious* means very *bad*; description: lesser degree
120. 1. c; Something *unique* is not a *facsimile*; object : description (reversed)
     2. a; A *lynx* is a kind of *feline*; object : category
121. 1. b; *Dribble* is a lesser degree of *spew*.
     2. c; *Elastic* is the same as *pliant*.
122. 1. e; To *undermine* someone's *confidence* is to diminish it over time.
     2. d; A *scam* is, by definition, *deceptive*.
123. 1. jeopardize; To *minimize* is the opposite of *aggrandize*.
     2. e; A *lair* is a type of *habitat*.
124. 1. a; To *implore* is to *plead*; word : synonym
     2. c; *Kinetic* means relating to *motion*.
125. 1. d; A *centennial* is a kind of *anniversary*.
     2. b; *Porous* is the opposite of *impermeable*.
126. 1. b; A *peccadillo* is a minor *argument*; object : greater degree
     2. a; A *contusion* is a *bruise*.
127. 1. d; *Obscure* describes a *fact* that is not well known.

Daily Warm-Ups: Analogies

2. e; *Logic*, by definition, is *cogent*.

128. 1. c; Someone *indecisive* is unable to *choose*.
2. a; A *dilemma* is a difficult *choice*.

129. 1. fierce; 2. migratory; 3. livid; 4. lithe;
5. smoldering

130. 1. e; *Proud* is the same as *haughty*; word : synonym
2. b; *Predilection* is the opposite of *distaste*; word : antonym

131. 1. d; To *sense* is to be *aware*.
2. c; Something *sensible* is something one can *perceive*.

132. 1. e; To *wheedle* is to *cajole*.
2. b; To *sway* an *opinion* is to change it.

133. 1. c; *Nefarious* describes a *malefactor*; person : description (reversed)
2. d; The job of a *champion* is to *advocate*; agent : action

134. 1. a; *Exhilaration* is a greater degree of *glee*.
2. b; *Jubilation* is an expression of *joy*.

135. 1. e; A *magnate* is characterized by *power*.
2. b; A *circuitous route* is indirect.

136. 1. b; A *teacher* is *didactic*.
2. d; A *dilettante* lacks *focus*.

137. 1. c; The function of a *garland* is to *festoon*; object : function
2. a; *Rococo* is the same as *ornate*; word : synonym

138. 1. a; A *yurt* is a type of *dwelling*; object : category
2. e; *Domesticated* is the opposite of *feral*; word : antonym

139. 1. b; *Police* operate within their *precinct*.
2. e; Someone *methodical* lacks *imprecision*.

140. 1. d; An *inquiry* is the same as a *query*.
2. a; Something *opaque* lacks *translucence*.

141. 1. c; The function of an *emollient* is to *soften*; object : function
2. b; A *panoramic* view is complete.

142. 1. a; To *stupefy* is to *astound*.
2. b; Something *independent* is not *shackled*.

143. 1. idiosyncratic; Someone *importunate* is *demanding*.
2. c; *Eager* is a lesser degree of *rapacious*.

144. 1. c; The action of a *pugilist* is to *fight*; agent : action
2. a; *Bellicose* is the opposite of *peaceable*; word : antonym

145. 1. d; agent : action; The action of a *captor* is to *encage*.

Daily Warm-Ups: Analogies

2. a; object : function; The purpose of a *trap* is to *ensnare*.

146. 1. e; *Torpid* is the same as *sluggish*.
2. b; The purpose of an *inoculation* is to cause *immunity*.

147. 1. d; A *braggart* lacks *humility*.
2. e; Someone with a great deal of *assurance* is *conceited*.

148. 1. a; *Mellifluous* is the opposite of *grating*; word : antonym
2. c; A *traitor* commits *treason*; agent : action

149. 1. d; *Hirsute* is the opposite of *hairless*.
2. b; A *receding tide* is diminishing.

150. 1. e; Something *ephemeral* lacks *longevity*.
2. a; *Stamina* is the same as *endurance*.

151. 1. c; *Dense fog* is very thick.
2. b; *Sparse* is a lesser degree of *barren*; description : greater degree

152. 1. d; To *begin* is the function of an *initiator*; agent : action
2. c; An *inauguration* is a type of *ceremony*; object : category

153. 1. a; Answers will vary but might be b, c, or e.

2. c; agent : action

154. 1. d; A *rarity* by definition is not *ubiquitous*.
2. b; *Rib* is a lesser degree of *ridicule*; action : greater degree

155. 1. culpable; person : description (reversed)
2. d; object : description

156. 1. e; Someone who is *repentant* has *contrition*.
2. c; Someone *rueful* has *regret*.

157. 1. b; person : description (reversed); Somebody who is *craven* is a *coward*.
2. a; object : greater size; A *tremor* is a smaller version of a *quake*.

158. 1. d; *Sedition* is a form of *rebellion*.
2. c; *Ascension* is the opposite of *decline*.

159. 1. a; object: function; The function of an *antiseptic* is to *sterilize*.
2. c; person : description; A *criminal* is *felonious*.

160. 1. d; object : function; The function of a *barricade* is to *block*.
2. e; word : synonym; *Portentous* is the same as *weighty*.

161. 1. d; *Alacrity* is the opposite of *hesitation*.
2. c; To be *pensive* is to *mull*.

Daily Warm-Ups: Analogies

162. 1. a; An *accord* is the opposite of a *disagreement*;
         word : antonym
      2. e; An *assenter concurs*; agent : action
163. 1. b; *Risky* is a lesser version of *perilous*; description
         : greater degree;
      2. e; *Inclement* describes very bad *weather*.
164. 1. a; Someone *illustrious* is characterized by
         eminence.
      2. c; A *master* is someone *accomplished*.
165. 1. e; *Delivery* is the job of a *courier*; agent : action
         (reversed)
      2. b; To *truncate* a *limb* is to shorten it.
166. 1. a; *Might* is the opposite of *frailty*.
      2. c; To *infringe* on someone's *right* is to violate it.
167. 1. c; *Ambivalence* is characterized by *contradiction*.
      2. e; A *manifesto* is a type of *declaration*.
168. 1. d; A *banquet* is a larger version of a *meal*; object :
         lesser degree
      2. c; An *apex* is the opposite of a *nadir*.
169. 1. b; To *condense* something causes a *reduction*;
         cause : effect
      2. b; A *cacophony* by definition is *discordant*; object
         : description

170. 1. a; *Ebullient* means the same as *effervescent*.
      2. b; Someone *oblivious* lacks *awareness*.
171. 1. d; A *din* is a large *noise*; object : lesser degree
      2. e; The action of a *proselytizer* is to *convert*; agent
         : action.
172. 1. e; To *quench thirst* is to relieve it.
      2. c; *Mitigation* is the opposite action as to
         exacerbate.
173. 1. a; adjective
      2. d; agent : action
174. 1. c; *Archaic* is the opposite of *modern*.
      2. b; A *labyrinth* is characterized by *intricacy*.
175. 1. a; *Pepper* is a kind of *spice*; object : category
      2. e; A *confection* is by definition *sweet*; object :
         description
176. 1. e; A *ban* is a prohibition of *goods*.
      2. b; *Culinary* means relating to *food*.
177. 1. d; A *fallacy* by definition is *erroneous*.
      2. c; To *err* is to make a *mistake*.
178. 1. a; To *fleece* is to *swindle*; word : synonym
      2. a; A *mishap* is a lesser version of a *catastrophe*;
         object : greater degree
179. 1. e; *Gratuitous* is the opposite of *costly*; word :

antonym
2. b; *Exorbitant* means extremely *expensive*;
   description : lesser degree

180. 1. c; *Ultimate* is the opposite of *initial*.
      2. a; A *meandering* road is *indirect*.